What Made Korea's R Growth Possible?

Korea's experience of rapid economic growth represents both hope and a challenge to many developing countries. The conventional wisdom inside and outside Korea has been that the government's policies such as export promotion, industrial targeting, and so on, made the rapid growth possible.

This book investigates the effects of the policies and concludes that Korea's growth experience does not corroborate the view. Rather, it points to the tremendous growth in size of the world market as an important factor that has been overlooked in the discussion of nations' economic growth in the post-World War II era. It was roughly 100 times bigger in the early 1960s than it was in the middle of the First Industrial Revolution. The potential "gains from trade" were that much greater; while the Korean economy had not been realizing the potential gains, it began to as soon as a major reform of the foreign exchange system in 1961 removed the impediments to foreign trade. Explosive export expansion and rapid growth of the economy immediately followed. The "Korean Miracle" may be better understood as a process whereby the economy realized its huge potential.

Jungho Yoo is Visiting Professor at the Korea Development Institute (KDI) School of Public Policy and Management, South Korea. He was previously Fellow at the KDI.

Routledge Studies in the Modern World Economy

For more information about this series, please visit www.routledge.com/ Routledge-Studies-in-the-Modern-World-Economy/book-series/SE0432

What Made Korea's Rapid Growth Possible?

Jungho Yoo

Routledge
Taylor & Francis Group
LONDON AND NEW YORK

First published 2020 by Routledge

2 Park Square, Milton Park, Abingdon, Oxon OX14 4RN

605 Third Avenue, New York, NY 10017

*Routledge is an imprint of the Taylor & Francis Group,
an informa business*

First issued in paperback 2022

British Library Cataloguing-in-Publication Data
A catalogue record for this book is available from the British Library

Library of Congress Cataloging-in-Publication Data
Names: Yoo, Jung-ho, author.
Title: What made Korea's rapid growth possible?/Jungho Yoo.
Description: Abingdon, Oxon; New York, NY: Routledge, 2020. |
Series: Routledge studies in the modern world economy |
Includes bibliographical references and index.
Identifiers: LCCN 2019051333 (print) | LCCN 2019051334 (ebook) |
ISBN 9781138801264 (hbk) | ISBN 9781315755052 (ebk)
Subjects: LCSH: Korea (South)–Economic conditions. |
Korea (South)–Economic policy. | Foreign exchange–Korea (South)
Classification: LCC HC467 .Y685 2020 (print) |
LCC HC467 (ebook) | DDC 330.95195–dc23
LC record available at https://lccn.loc.gov/2019051333
LC ebook record available at https://lccn.loc.gov/2019051334

ISBN: 978-1-138-80126-4 (hbk)
ISBN: 978-1-03-233691-6 (pbk)
DOI: 10.4324/9781315755052

Typeset in ITC Galliard Std
by Newgen Publishing UK

To my dear wife, Inwon

Contents

Figures

Tables

Preface

The Republic of Korea (Korea, hereafter) was one of the poorest countries in the world in the early 1960s. The land area is small with few natural resources and only 20 percent is arable; the population density is the third-highest among those countries with a population of 10 million or more; the level of science and technology was at the time far behind that of other countries. In the late 1990s, Korea became a member country of the Organisation for Economic Co-operation and Development (OECD), the rich countries' club; in 2017, the economy was the fourteenth-largest in the world and the fifth-largest exporter. Thus, Korea represents hope and a challenge to many developing countries. If Korea made it, there is no reason why other countries cannot.

Yet, what made Korea's rapid economic growth possible, especially concerning the role of the government, is still an unsettled question. Regarding policies at the macro level, which more or less equally affect all industries and economic agents in the economy, there is broad agreement. The Korean government provided macroeconomic stability, made investments in infrastructure and human capital, and maintained outward orientation in its economic policies, and so on, and its role was indispensable to the economy's rapid growth and industrialization. However, there are widely different views regarding the effects of policies at industry level that affected individual industries (and/or firms) differently, which may be called "intervention" in the market.

Many inside and outside Korea hold the view that such interventionist policies were the key cause of the rapid economic growth and industrialization. Indeed, Korea's development experience is often characterized as "government-led". Were the interventionist policies the main reason for Korea's rapid growth and industrialization? If not, what was? These are the questions this book addresses. It does not intend to provide a comprehensive review of Korea's economic development. In particular, it does not discuss the policies at the macroeconomic level or their effects. The focus is narrow. It mainly examines the effects of the exchange rate policy of the 1950s and the trade and industrial policies of the 1960s and 1970s to determine whether Korea's growth experience corroborates the widely held view regarding interventionist policies as the driver of rapid economic growth.

Concerning this question, my own research findings point to the size of the world market. The world market was more than 100 times bigger in the early 1960s, when Korea was beginning to industrialize, than in 1820, when European economies were in the middle of the First Industrial Revolution. Because of this difference in the size of the world market, international trade played an incomparably bigger role in Korea's economic growth and industrialization than it had in the growth and industrialization of European countries. Of course, a country does not get the benefits of international trade if it does not engage in international trade, however big the world market may be.

1 The economy and policies in the 1950s

1.1 The Korean economy

In 1945, as World War II came to an end, Korea was liberated from Japanese colonial rule and the Korean peninsula was divided into two along the 38th parallel. The South was occupied by the United States, the North by the Soviet Union. In 1948, the governments of both North and South Korea came into being. In 1950, the Korean War broke out; an armistice agreement was reached in 1953.[1]

At the time of partition, roughly two-thirds of the population of the peninsula were living in the South (17.0 million) and one-third in the North (8.9 million). Between 1945 and 1949, due to the massive repatriation of overseas Koreans (1.41 million from Japan and 0.62 million from Manchuria) and refugees from the North (0.46 million), the population of the South increased by 2.48 million. The North had a slightly larger surface area (120,000 square kilometers) than the South (100,000 square kilometers), with arable land accounting for about 20 percent of the total in each. Of the arable land in the South, 60 percent was rice paddies and the rest dry fields; in the North, 23.5 percent was rice paddies and the rest dry fields.

Most of the peninsula's mineral resources were located in the North, and nearly all electric power (92 percent) was generated in the North. The manufacturing sector was small for the whole peninsula, while the industrial structures of the South and the North were highly complementary to each other. Most heavy industries were located in the North, with most light industries in the South. In 1940, the North produced about 90 percent of the country's total metal products and 83 percent of its chemical products; the South produced 85 percent of textiles, 72 percent of machinery and 64 percent of the processed food output. According to the statistics from 1940, the total "net commodity-product" (defined as the net-value output of the agriculture, forestry, fishery, mining, and manufacturing sectors, which excludes double-counting[2]) in the South was slightly greater than in the North. However, in per-capita terms, the net commodity-product was 60 percent greater in the North, as the South had twice as large a population as the North.[3]

Under the 35-year Japanese rule, the economy had been dominated by Japanese firms, capital, and technicians. In the late 1930s, Japanese residents made up only 3 percent of the total Korean population. However, Japanese-controlled businesses accounted for 58 percent of the total of 5,413 establishments and 89 percent of the paid-in capital of all business establishments, implying that in terms of paid-in capital the Japanese firms were on average nearly six times larger than Korean firms. In 1944, Japanese engineers and technicians in manufacturing, construction, and public utilities accounted for 80 percent of the total.

The Liberation in 1945 meant a sudden separation of the economy from the Japanese economic bloc, as well as partition of the country. Economic chaos followed. By the next year, the number of manufacturing establishments dropped by half and manufacturing employment by 60 percent in the South. Additionally, a severe food shortage developed, and hyper-inflation was set off by uncontrolled expansion of the money supply before and after the Liberation; "The Seoul retail price index increased about 123 times from June 1945 to June 1949."[4]

In 1948, the North completely and finally shut off the power supply to the South, immediately creating a serious power shortage. The Korean War broke out in June 1950, ending in 1953. Roughly 1 million civilians were killed or wounded during the war, with 137,000 South Korean soldiers and around 40,000 UN soldiers killed in action. The war damage to South Korea is estimated to have been equal to 86 percent of a year's gross national product (GNP) in 1953.[5]

Statistics on the Korean economy in the South are scanty for the years immediately following the Liberation and during the period of Korean War. No national income estimate is available. The first year for which consistent national income account data are available is 1953, the year the Korean War ended. The subsequent years until 1957 are considered the recovery period, during which the growth rate of the economy was relatively rapid. Afterwards, the growth rate declined from 6.1 percent in 1958 to 4.6 percent in 1959 and 1.8 percent in 1960, mostly because of a forcefully applied financial stabilization program. Available statistics indicate that the "net commodity-product for 1953 was about 27 percent lower than that for 1940".[6] If the ratio of GNP to net commodity-product in 1953 had been the same as it was in 1940, GNP in 1953 must also have been 27 percent lower than it was in 1940. If that had been the case, and GNP had grown at the rates shown in Table 1.1, GNP slightly exceeded the 1940 level for the first time in 1961: a loss of 20 years of economic growth.

Foreign trade was not important to the Korean economy at the time. From the Liberation to the end of the Korean War, private foreign trade had been almost non-existent; some barter trade took place. The government was the major exporter of such products as tungsten or ginseng. As Table 1.2 shows, in the second half of the 1950s, total exports averaged around 20 million dollars per year, mostly of agricultural, fishery, and mineral products. Total imports averaged around 370 million dollars, roughly 80 percent of which was

Table 1.1 Growth and inflation rates, 1954–1970 (%)

	GNP	WPI	Seoul CPI
1954	6.0	n.a.	n.a.
1955	6.3	n.a.	n.a.
1956	1.3	31.7	23.0
1957	7.2	16.1	23.2
1958	6.1	–6.1	–3.6
1959	4.6	2.3	3.2
1960	1.8	10.8	8.1
1961	4.8	13.2	8.2
1962	3.5	9.4	6.6
1963	9.1	20.6	20.6
1964	8.3	34.6	29.6
1965	7.4	10.0	13.5
1966	13.4	8.9	12.0
1967	8.9	6.4	10.9
1968	12.6	8.1	11.2
1969	15.0	6.8	10.0
1970	7.9	9.2	12.7

Source: Bank of Korea, *Economic Statistics Yearbook* 1965, 1970, 1972.

Notes: The growth rates of GNP are derived by the author from the estimates of GNP in varying constant prices: 1960 constant won for 1954–1963, 1965 constant won for 1964–1968, and 1970 constant won for 1969–1970. Inflation rates by WPI and Seoul CPI are derived by the author from the corresponding price indices. n.a.= not available.

foreign aid, mostly inflows of relief from the US such as food, coal, oil, textiles, fertilizers, etc., intended to provide the population with sustenance and to restore basic economic functions. The trade account was always in large deficit in the 1950s. Merchandise exports remained much less than 1 percent of GNP. Since the outbreak of the Korean War in 1950, aid had arrived through multi-lateral channels, such as Civil Relief in Korea(CRIK) and the United Nations Korea Reconstruction Agency (UNKRA), which in any case came mostly from the US.

The rest of this chapter briefly reviews the government policies on exchange rates and trade in the 1950sas the background materials for the next chapter, which will discuss the major reform of the foreign exchange system in 1961 and how Korea's rapid export expansion began and continued into the next decade.

1.2 The exchange rate policy in the 1950s

This section considers the evolution of the exchange rate between the Korean won and the US dollar in the 1950s. The won–dollar exchange rate began, "set at 0.015 won to one U.S. dollar in October 1945, equivalent to the yen exchange

Table 1.2 Merchandise exports, imports, and aid, 1945–1963 (in million current dollars)

	Exports	Imports	Aid	Foreign exchange reserves
1945			4.9	
1946			49.5	
1947			175.4	
1948			179.6	
1949			116.5	
1950			58.7	
1951			106.5	
1952	27.7	214.2	161.3 (75.3)	n.a.
1953	39.6	345.4	194.2 (56.2)	109.0
1954	24.2	243.3	153.9 (63.3)	108.0
1955	18.0	341.4	236.7 (69.3)	96.0
1956	24.6	386.1	326.7 (84.6)	99.0
1957	22.2	442.2	382.9 (86.6)	116.0
1958	16.5	378.2	321.3 (85.0)	146.0
1959	19.8	303.8	222.2 (73.1)	147.0
1960	32.8	343.5	245.4 (71.4)	157.0
1961	40.9	316.1	199.2 (63.0)	207.0
1962	54.8	421.8	232.3 (55.1)	169.0
1963	86.8	560.3	216.4 (38.6)	131.0

Source: Bank of Korea, *Economics Statistics Yearbook* 1960, 1970.

Notes: Exports and imports for 1951 and earlier years are not shown, as consistent statistics are not available. The numbers in the parentheses are the aids as a percentage of total imports. Foreign exchange reserves include gold holdings.

rate in Japan".[7] The rate applied mostly to settlements of US military government liabilities against the private sector and other minor transactions. It had little to do with trade, as private foreign trade was almost non-existent at the time. Then, in July 1950, shortly after the outbreak of the Korean War, an agreement was made between the Korean and US governments to help the UN forces dispatched to the Korean peninsula to carry out their mission. Under the agreement, commonly called the "won advance agreement", the Korean government would advance won to United Nations Command (UNC) for its expenditures in Korea, to be paid back in dollars.[8,9]

The agreement determined the direction of the exchange rate policy for the rest of the decade. Throughout the 1950s, despite rampant inflation, the official exchange rate was kept low and devaluation was delayed as long as possible, obviously to maximize the dollar receipt for a given amount of won advance. The lower the won–dollar exchange rate, the greater the amount of the dollars received. The dollars thus received were the most important source of foreign exchanges during the Korean War.[10] Prior to the agreement, the monetary authority was apparently concerned with overvaluation of won due to inflation. A bidding system was introduced and was in operation until the outbreak of the Korean War, for example. The record shows that in a span of two years from August 1948, when the Korean government was established, to July 1950, when the won advance agreement was made, there were four devaluations. In comparison, only four devaluations took place in the next ten years since the agreement until February 1960.[11]

The won advance agreement was a source of conflict between the two governments. From the US point of view the official exchange rate applied to redemption was unrealistically low. For example, the official rate was 2.5 won to the dollar and the curb market rate was 3.42 won to the dollar on November 1, 1950; the official rate was 6.0 won to the dollar in November 10, 1951, while the curb market rate was 18.21 won to the dollar.[12] On the other hand, the Korean government was concerned with the increase in money supply due to the won advances and the consequent inflation. The US delayed the dollar payments for won advanced—the first won advance was made in July 1950, and the first redemption of won advances was made in October 1951 but not fully until May 1952. Meanwhile, the money supply multiplied four times during the one-year period after the agreement, and the consumer price hiked roughly five times in Busan, the temporary capital city during the Korean War.[13] Under the circumstances a low exchange rate was considered an effective tool in controlling inflation, for aggregate supply could be increased by increasing imports with the dollars received through the redemption, whereas it was nearly impossible to increase the aggregate supply through production in wartime.

The Korean and US governments came to an agreement over the official exchange rate in December 1953, the first one since the outbreak of the Korean War, and set the rate at 18 won to the dollar. This rate was soon threatened by inflation and also by the worsening prospect of exports, rising bilateral trade deficits with Japan, and rumors of American troop withdrawal. In August 1954 the rate in the market was hovering above 50 won to the dollar, and the US government demanded a rate increase. But the two governments could not reach an agreement, and the US government delayed dollar repayment. In response the Korean government discontinued won advances in October 1954, and the US government stopped the supply of petroleum products for civilian use. The stalemate was resolved on November 11, 1954 by an agreement that the UNC would procure won by the auction sale of dollars, while leaving the official rate unchanged at 18 won to the dollar.

Soon the bidding rate shot above the official exchange rate. In August 1955 it reached 72.9 won to the dollar. Eventually the two governments agreed to the official rate of 50 won to the dollar, effective August 1955. On this occasion it was decided to discontinue the bidding and that the US would sell the dollars to the Bank of Korea at the official exchange rate, which was in the future to be determined by referring to the wholesale price index of Seoul, with September 1955 as the base period. The official rate was going to rise or fall, as the price index rose or fell by more than 25 percent than that of the base period.

After a relatively long period of price stability, the wholesale price index, which was 100 in 1955, reached 130.2 in 1959. The US government requested a consultation in January 1960, but the Korean government wanted to delay. Then, on January 29, the US embassy in Seoul unilaterally decided to use the exchange rate of 65 won to the dollar as an internal administrative measure, which was 30 percent higher than the ongoing rate. The Korean government, following a consultation with the IMF, announced the new exchange rate in February 1960 of 65 won to the dollar.

In less than two months, the Student Revolution of April 1960 ousted the Syngman Rhee government, the first government since Independence. Because of this, the official relationship of aid and economic cooperation between the Korean and US governments, excluding military aid, was temporarily discontinued. On the occasion of resuming the relationship some time in the same year, the US government suggested an increase in the exchange rate, which led to the announcement in October by the then-newly elected Chang Myon government of a new exchange rate of 100 won to the dollar, effective January 1, 1961. The next month, February 1961, the new government once again devalued won on its own initiative by raising the exchange rate to 130 won to the dollar, as part of a major reform of the foreign exchange system that abolished the multiple exchange rates and adopted a uniform rate (to be discussed in the next chapter). Thus, three consecutive devaluations in a span of one year from February 1960 to February 1961 raised the exchange rate from 50 to 130 won to the dollar, nearly wiping out the overvaluation of won.

1.3 Foreign exchange control and multiple exchange rates

As was noted at the outset of this chapter, the trade account was always in big deficit in the 1950s, and the foreign exchange shortage was severe. Imports were around 18 times as large as the meager exports in the second half of the decade and were mostly financed by aid. Also, as was noted in the previous section, the government kept the official exchange rate unrealistically low throughout the decade, and won remained highly overvalued. Thus, the official exchange rate played no role as a price variable in equating the demand for and supply of foreign exchange. Not surprisingly, strict control of foreign exchange was considered inevitable, and a very complicated structure of foreign exchange rates consequently emerged.

The Bank of Korea, established in June 1950, managed the foreign exchange control system. The Bank was the only financial institution that could legally handle transactions in foreign exchanges, and all privately held foreign exchanges had to be deposited at the Bank of Korea under the "foreign exchange deposit system". There were three different kinds of private deposit accounts: export, general, and special. Export accounts were maintained by individuals or firms directly engaged in export and import business, general accounts were opened mainly by foreign diplomatic personnel, and special accounts were used by residents and non-residents who were not authorized to open an export or general account. In August 1955 the accounts were consolidated by introducing "import accounts", which absorbed the export and special accounts, while general accounts remained the same.

There were two main sources of foreign exchanges in the years following the end of the Korean War: aid dollars from the US and UNKRA and the foreign exchanges held by the Korean government, known as KFX.[14] The latter were mostly composed of the redemption dollars the Korean government received for the won advances and the proceeds from the government's export of tungsten, ginseng, etc. They had to be allocated to private traders and end-users of imports of raw materials, investment goods, and so on. Since the official exchange rate did not function as a price variable, various schemes had to be used for the purpose of foreign exchange allocation. Hence, a complicated structure of multiple foreign exchange rates came into being.

From December 1952 to July 1954 the allocation scheme of KFX was "special foreign exchange loans", which financed about 45 percent of total imports (or 75 percent of private imports). The scheme had two kinds of loan: the first was allocated to exporters and raw material end-users on the basis of export performance and raw material needs; the second was allocated to major domestic industries for imports of capital goods. The loans were to be repaid in dollars when due, and the borrowers were required to make an initial deposit at the Bank of Korea in won equal to the loan. The exchange rates applied for this purpose to the two different kinds of loan were not the same. For example, the rates applied to the first kind of loan ranged from 15.5 to 29.6 won to the dollar from November 1952 until the end of the war in 1953, while the official exchange rate of 6.0 won to the dollar was applied to the second kind of loan. Moreover, the exchange rates applied to individual loans differed, depending on the ratio of domestic over foreign price of the imports, for which the dollar was used. Applying the same rate to all would have meant a bigger profit for importers of those products for which the domestic price to foreign price ratio was higher, which could be regarded as an "unfair" privilege.

From October 1954 to August 1955 competitive bidding was used to allocate foreign exchange. The bidding rate in 1954 ranged from 46.1 to 69.3 won to the dollar, while the official rate remained at 18. From August 1955 to May 1957 a lottery was used; from May 1957 to August 1958 a modified bidding system was used, with priority given to those who were willing to purchase the most national bonds in addition to won deposits at the official exchange rate. After August 1958 a combined foreign exchange tax and bidding system was used. Under the system, a basic tax of 15 won to the dollar was required on all foreign exchange purchases and the foreign exchanges for commercial imports were allocated to those who paid the most additional tax above the basic rate, a kind of competitive bidding.

While the proceeds from private exports represented a very small part of the total supply of foreign exchanges, there still arose a separate exchange rate for exporters, called a "transfer rate". The foreign exchange deposit system mentioned above required all privately held foreign exchanges be deposited with the Bank of Korea. Accordingly, exporters had accounts denominated in foreign currencies with the Bank of Korea and sold their foreign exchange earnings by transferring the balances in their accounts to accounts of other traders. This gave rise to "transfer rates", which were much higher than the official exchange rate. Moreover, the rates differed depending on where the foreign exchanges were earned; the transfer rates on "Japan export dollars", the dollars earned from exports to Japan, were higher than the rates on "Other export dollars", which were earned from exports to other regions. Imports from Japan were more restricted, hence more profitable, and only dollars earned in Japan were allowed to be used for importing goods from Japan, which was a policy measure to contain the large bilateral trade deficit with Japan.

1.4 Trade policies in the 1950s

Before the Korean government came into being in 1948, the US military government instituted an import and export licensing system in 1946, under which the government simply announced the items that could be licensed for import and those that were prohibited. Export was also under control, the main goal being to discourage exports of "essential goods" and to prevent capital flights. The tariffs were set at a uniform rate of 10 percent on all goods except those financed by foreign assistance.

1.4.1 Import policy

The newly established Korean government introduced an import quota system in 1949; it specified not only the items that could be imported, but also the quantities. In 1955 a trade program replaced the import quota system. Under the new system, importable goods were divided into automatically approved, restricted, and prohibited ones. If domestic production of some goods was sufficient for domestic demand, import of those goods was prohibited; if domestic production was less than sufficient, import of those goods was permitted but restricted. The Ministry of Commerce and Industry had the discretion to allow imports of prohibited or restricted items. In the second half of the 1950s the percentage of automatically approved items—those that could be imported without prior government approval—was always much less than 10 percent of total importable items.

In 1950 the Korean government changed the tariff system set in 1946 in order to increase tariff revenue, on the one hand, and to encourage domestic production, on the other. The average tariff rate rose to 40 percent, and tariff escalation was introduced. The tariff rate ranged from 0 percent on such essential goods as food grains and non-competing capital goods to more than 100 percent on luxury goods. The rate on those goods that would compete with domestically produced goods was higher than for other categories. The tariff rate was also higher on "finished goods" that needed no further processing before final use than on "unfinished" goods that required further processing in the domestic economy before final use.

The import policy clearly intended to protect and encourage domestic industries. Indeed, it was an integral part of the government's development policy in the 1950s, the aim of which was industrialization through import substitution under protection. In 1952 the government introduced tariff exemptions on imports of capital goods for certain major industries, including electric power, shipbuilding, metal working, machinery, chemicals, oil refining, textiles, mining, and fishing. However, the tariff structure remained basically unaltered until the early 1970s.

1.4.2 Export promotion measures

While the trade policy in the main was protectionist, the government took a number of measures to promote export in the 1950s to deal with the severe shortage of foreign exchange. An "export credit system" (earlier known as a "trade credit system") had been in place since 1950, under which exporters enjoyed priority in the allocation of domestic credits; the loans made to them were not bound by quarterly credit ceilings, a measure of anti-inflationary monetary policy at the time. From 1952 to 1954 exporters enjoyed "preferential access to special foreign exchange loans", a scheme that allocated KFX, discussed in the previous subsection. The "preferential export system", also known as the "export–import link system", was adopted in 1951, under which exporters of so-called nonessential products enjoyed the right to use from 1 to 10 percent (from 4 to 50 percent after 1953) of their foreign exchange earnings for importing popular items, which otherwise could not be imported. As import was under quantitative control, the import permits no doubt meant an increase in earnings for the exporters. The system was discontinued in August 1955, at the time of devaluation.[15]

In 1954 a "direct subsidy" was provided for exporters but was discontinued the next year, as the government failed to provide for it in the budget. The subsidy was reinstituted in 1961 and continued until the time of extensive devaluation in 1964.[16] The "traders' licensing system" under the Trade Transactions Law of 1957 included an implicit encouragement of export, as it required export performance for traders to be licensed, and the requirement was more lenient for exporters than for importers.[17] "Tariff exemption" was introduced in 1959 on imports of raw materials and intermediate goods for export, and later also on capital equipment for export(to be changed to "tariff rebate" in 1974).[18]

Notes

1 This chapter draws upon Frank, Kim, and Westphal (1975), Kim and Westphal (1976), and Kim and Roemer (1979) for factual information.
2 Kim and Roemer (1979), pp. 8–9.
3 Kim and Roemer (1979), Table 12, p. 23.
4 Kim and Westphal (1976), p. 30.
5 Kim and Roemer (1979), p. 31.
6 Kim and Roemer (1979), p. 36. The source adds that "... this comparison can only indicate very roughly the magnitude of change in net commodity-product during the period".
7 The exchange rate is expressed in current won, the Korean currency that has had two currency reforms since then: a 100:1 revaluation in 1953 and another one of 10:1 in 1961. Frank, Kim, and Westphal (1975), p. 28.
8 The official name was "Agreement between the Government of U.S.A. and the Republic of Korea Government Regarding Expenditures by Forces under Command of the Commanding General, Armed Forces of Member States of the United Nations". See Frank, Kim, and Westphal (1975), p. 28.
9 This section draws heavily upon Bank of Korea (1960) for factual information.
10 "Foreign exchange from this source amounted to $62 million in 1952 and $122 million in 1953, or about 62 and 70 percent of total foreign exchange receipts in those years." See Frank, Kim, and Westphal (1975), p. 28.
11 Bank of Korea (1960).
12 Frank, Kim, and Westphal (1975), Table 3.1, pp. 30–31.
13 Bank of Korea (1960), p. 15.
14 UNKRA and US aid financed approximately 1.9 billion dollars of imports, or about 72 percent of total imports from 1953 to 1960. Frank, Kim, and Westphal (1975), p. 29.
15 Kim and Westphal (1976), pp. 42 and 59. Non-essential products included star-fish, dolls, lacquer-wares, etc.
16 Hong (1979), p. 49. See also Kim and Westphal (1976), p. 69.
17 Frank, Kim, and Westphal (1975), p. 39
18 Kim and Westphal (1976), pp. 64 and 70.

References

Bank of Korea, 1965, *Economic Statistics Yearbook*, various issues. Seoul: The Bank of Korea.

Bank of Korea, Research Department, 1960, "Changes in Official Exchange Rate", *Bank of Korea Research Monthly*, December, Vol. 14, pp. 12–24 (in Korean).

Frank, Charles R., Jr., Kwang Suk Kim, and Larry E. Westphal, 1975, *Foreign Trade Regimes and Economic Development: South Korea*, New York: National Bureau of Economic Research.

Hong, Wontack, 1979, *Trade, Distortions and Employment Growth in Korea*, Seoul: Korea Development Institute.

Kim, Kwang Suk and Michael Roemer, 1979, *Growth and Structural Transformation*, Cambridge, MA: Council on East Asian Studies, Harvard University.

Kim, Kwang Suk and Larry E. Westphal, 1976, *Korea's Foreign Exchange and Trade Regimes*, Seoul: KDI (in Korean).

2 Rapid export expansion in the 1960s and 1970s

Korea's merchandise exports began to suddenly and rapidly expand in the early 1960s, and this rapid expansion continued into the following decades. In real terms the average annual growth rate of export was 35.3 percent for 1963–1969 and 25.4 percent in the 1970s. Undoubtedly, this rapid export expansion was a very important reason for the economy's rapid growth, which was on average nearly 10 percent per annum for the same period.[1]

However, when, how, and why the rapid export expansion began has not been clearly accounted for until recently. Most of the early studies of Korea's economic growth tend to attribute the export success to the government policy of export promotion that started in the mid-1960s.[2] On the other hand, studies that have appeared since the late 1980s hold different views regarding the export success, growth, and industrialization in general. They tend to attribute the success to the government's industrial policies, including the provision of credit subsidies, tax incentives, administrative guidance, etc. For example, one author claims that the coordination failure that had been blocking Korea's economic growth was remedied by such government intervention, and an investment boom and a rise in imports followed—the conclusion being that it was this increase in imports that led to export expansion.[3]

This chapter discusses how rapid export expansion began and continued into the 1970s. Factual information on the policy measures to be discussed in this chapter comes mostly from the early studies mentioned above. This chapter also draws on statistics, writings, and other information that have been in the public domain and examines the details. The section "The beginning of rapid export expansion" dates the beginning of the rapid export expansion. The section "How the rapid export expansion began" finds the reason for the beginning in the major reform of the foreign exchange system in 1961, which abolished the multiple exchange rates and adopted one uniform and realistic exchange rate. This goes against the views held by the early studies, as well as those of the later studies mentioned above. The section "Export success and export promotion" discusses the evidence suggesting that the export promotion policy was inspired by the rapid export expansion itself. Finally, the section "Export promotion and its effects" discusses the effect of the government's export promotion policy on export.

2.1 The beginning of rapid export expansion

In investigating how and why rapid export expansion began, the first task is to date its beginning. It will then become clear where to look for the cause, which, be it a change in policy or in circumstance, is to be found before the beginning, not after. The attempt to date the beginning of a country's export expansion may sound nonsensical, for trade must have been going on since time immemorial between regions and across borders. What this section intends to do is to date the beginning of Korea's "rapid" export expansion, and it makes eminent sense to do so in the Korean experience, as will become clear. For this purpose, this section looks at Korea's export trends from various angles.

The first thing to examine is the total merchandise exports, shown for 1957–1970 in Table 2.1. The total figure is broken into two groups, manufactures and others, and the last column shows the total as a percentage of GNP. The importance of export to the economy dramatically increased in the 1960s; it had been less than 1 percent of GNP in the late 1950s and rose to 10.2 percent by 1970.

From a quick glance at the table it looks as if 1959 may be considered the first year of rapid export expansion, for in that year the total export began to increase at double-digit rates. However, the growth of that year was due to a 25.5-percent increase in non-manufactures exports, which was not repeated in the following years. The unmistakable characteristic exhibited by Korea's export expansion in the subsequent years was that it was led by manufactures exports. Since 1960 manufactures exports had always grown much faster than non-manufactures exports, as Table 2.1 shows.

Table 2.1 Merchandise exports, 1957–1970 (in million current dollars)

	Total export			Export/GNP (%)
		Manufactures	*Non-manufactures*	
1957	22.2(−9.7)	4.1(66.6)	18.1(−18.2)	0.6
1958	16.5(−25.9)	2.6(−37.3)	13.9(−23.3)	0.6
1959	19.8(20.4)	2.4(−7.1)	17.4(25.5)	0.7
1960	32.8(65.7)	4.5(89.2)	28.3(62.5)	1.4
1961	40.9(24.5)	6.2(37.8)	34.6(22.4)	1.8
1962	54.8(34.1)	10.6(69.6)	44.2(27.5)	2.0
1963	86.8(58.4)	39.5(273.7)	47.3(6.6)	2.9
1964	119.1(37.2)	58.3(47.7)	60.7(28.9)	3.9
1965	175.1(47.1)	106.8(83.1)	68.3(12.5)	5.8
1966	250.3(43.0)	153.6(43.9)	96.7(41.6)	6.6
1967	320.2(27.9)	215.2(40.0)	105.1(8.7)	7.1
1968	455.4(42.2)	338.2(57.2)	117.2(11.6)	8.1
1969	622.5(36.7)	479.1(41.7)	143.4(22.3)	8.8
1970	835.2(34.2)	646.3(34.9)	188.9(31.8)	10.2

Source: KOSIS, online information service, National Statistical Office, the Korean government. www.kosis.kr.

Note: The numbers in the parentheses are annual growth rates in current dollars.

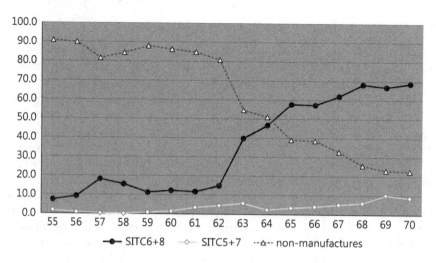

Figure 2.1 Export composition, 1955–1970.
Source: Table 2.A1.

Could 1960 be considered the first year of the rapid export expansion, then? Yes, if export of all manufactures should serve as the guide in dating the beginning. However, not all kinds of manufactured goods increased equally rapidly; a particular kind did. This can be seen in Figure 2.1, which decomposes manufactures exports into two subgroups: one comprising Standard International Trade Classification (SITC) 5, "chemicals", and SITC 7, "machinery and transport equipment"; the other comprises SITC 6, "manufactured goods chiefly classified by materials", and SITC 8, "miscellaneous manufactured articles". The subgroup "SITC6+8" consists mostly of labor-intensive goods, while "SITC5+7" consists mostly of capital-intensive goods, which also tend to be of more sophisticated production technology. The figure shows that the share of SITC 6+8 in total exports increased rapidly from around 10 percent in 1962 to nearly 70 percent in 1968. It is beyond any doubt that labor-intensive manufactures led the sudden and rapid expansion of Korea's exports in the 1960s. On this ground, 1962 may be determined the first year of the rapid export expansion.

Yet, there is still another peculiar feature that deserves attention: new export items appeared within subgroup SITC 6+8 and led the expansion, as can be seen in Table 2.A1 in the Appendix to this chapter. Striking in the table is the fact that exports of two-digit SITC or lower-level products belonging to SITC 6+8 were almost non-existent up to 1960, the exceptions being cotton fabrics and veneer sheets. This changed suddenly. After 1961 new export items began to appear in the subgroup: footwear, travel goods, and clothing in 1961; artificial flowers, synthetic fabrics, and umbrellas in 1962; woolen fabrics and wigs in 1963.

Table 2.2 shows that, once begun, exports of these new items increased incomparably faster than exports of then-existing items. From 1961 to 1965 the

Table 2.2 Export of new items, 1960–1970 (in thousand current dollars)

	1961	1962	1963	1964	1965	... 1970	Ratio (1965/ 1961)	Ratio (1970/ 1961)
New items	36 (0.09)	1,398 (2.55)	5,984 (6.89)	9,678 (8.13)	32,590 (18.6)	349,205 (41.8)	905.3	9,700.1
All other items	40,842	53,415	80,818	109,380	142,492	... 485,977	3.5	11.9

Source: Table 2.A1.

Notes: "New items" are footwear, travel goods, and clothing that began to appear in 1961; synthetic fabrics, umbrellas, and artificial flowers in 1962; woolen fabrics and wigs in 1963. Exports of "all other items" refers to the total export less exports of the new items. The numbers in the parentheses are percentage shares of new items in total exports.

exports of the new items multiplied more than 900 times, while the exports of all other items, namely, total exports less the exports of the new items, multiplied 3.5 times. By 1970 the exports of the same new items multiplied 9,700 times, while those of all other items multiplied 12 times. The most incredible example was clothing (SITC 84), export of which grew from 2,000 dollars in 1961 to 213.6 million dollars in 1970, a multiplication of more than 100,000 times in 9 years (Table 2.A1 in the Appendix to this chapter). In percentage terms the exports of all other items grew by an average of roughly 31 percent from 1961 to 1970, a very rapid growth—which, however, was growth at a "snail's pace" in comparison to the growth of new items. Of course, the explosive export growth of the new items could not continue indefinitely. The growth rate gradually slowed and approached that of all other items by 1969.

It was these new items that led the sudden and rapid export expansion of labor-intensive manufactures of SITC 6+8. As shown in Table 2.2, these new export items accounted for less than 0.1 percent of total exports in 1961 but 42 percent by 1970. It is little exaggeration to say that Korea's rapid export expansion in the 1960s was the expansion of these new items. For this reason, it seems appropriate to take 1961 as the year that marks beginning of Korea's rapid export expansion.

2.2 Trade and exchange rate policies

Now that the date for the beginning of rapid export expansion has been determined, this section examines official trade and exchange rate policies in search of the reason(s) for the start of the expansion.

2.2.1 Protectionist import policy

Korea's import policy was protectionist in the 1950s, being an integral part of the government's development strategy of industrialization through import substitution, and it remained so through the next decades until the early 1980s, when

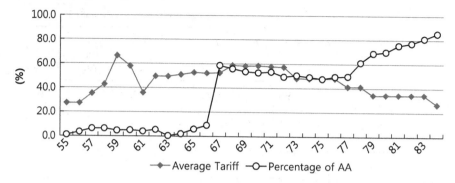

Figure 2.2 Graphic summary of import policy, 1955–1984.

Note: AA stands for automatic approval. AA items could be imported without prior government approval.

Source: Table 2.A2.

trade liberalization began in earnest.[4] The protectionist import policy is graphically summarized in Figure 2.2, which shows the average legal tariff rate and the percentage of automatic-approval (AA) items that could be imported without prior government approval from 1955 to the mid-1980s.

Until the mid-1960s AA items accounted for less than 10 percent of all imports. From 1967, when Korea joined the General Agreement on Tariffs and Trade (GATT), the proportion shot up but remained under 60 percent until the end of the 1970s. The average legal tariff rate was consistently around 50 percent for most of the 1960s and 1970s. Also, tariff escalation was built into the tariff system, as was mentioned in the previous chapter, which reflected the strategy of industrialization through import substitution.

The protectionist import policy of the 1950s could hardly have been the reason for the beginning of the rapid export expansion. As Lerner's Symmetry Theorem demonstrates, the imposition of tariffs on imports has an export-depressing effect, as it raises the price of the protected good relative to the export good, thereby making it more profitable to produce import-competing goods for the domestic market than to produce export goods for foreign markets.[5] Also, protection tends to reduce the value-added in export production by raising the prices of the protected intermediate inputs in the domestic market. Import restriction has an additional export-depressing effect through its effect on the foreign exchange rate; import restriction reduces import demand and, therefore, the demand for foreign exchanges, thereby lowering the exchange rate and discouraging exports.

2.2.2 Export promotion measures in the early 1960s

As noted above, in the 1950s the development strategy was basically industrialization through import substitution. However, the government tried various export promotion measures to deal with the severe shortage of foreign exchanges at the time. As was discussed in the previous chapter, the measures adopted in the 1950s and still in effect in the early 1960s were: an export credit system, exemption from commodity tax, tariff exemptions on imported inputs for exports, and the encouragement of exports implicit in a trader registration system. In the subsequent years some additional measures were adopted. A system of direct subsidies was reinstituted in 1961 but was discontinued in 1964 at the time of large devaluation.[6] In 1961 an income tax reduction of 30 percent was newly introduced for export earnings, which was raised to 50 percent the next year. The Korea Trade Promotion Corporation (KOTRA) was founded in 1962 to assist exporters in gathering information on and entering new foreign markets. In 1963, in response to an import surge and a rapid decline in foreign exchange reserves, the government instituted a full-scale "export–import link system", which gave exporters the right to use 100 percent of their export earnings for imports. The export–import link system was discontinued in May 1964, at the time of large devaluation. Also, the preferential interest rate on loans to exporters continued to be lowered from 1963, and the interest rate gap between ordinary loans and export loans widened thereafter, not closing until the early 1980s (see Table 4.3, Chapter 4).

To determine whether these export promotion measures were the reason for the start of the rapid export expansion, one would naturally turn to exporters' earnings that may have increased because of the measures. Fortunately, Frank, Kim, and Westphal (1975) have published estimates of exporters' earnings for 1958–1970, which they call "purchasing-power-parity effective exchange rate on exports".[7] The authors first estimate "effective exchange rate on exports", which is the sum of the official exchange rate, export dollar premium, and estimated subsidies per dollar exports. "Export dollar premium" is simply the excess of the market exchange rate over and above the official exchange rate, which had been always kept well below the market rate in the 1950s, as was discussed in the previous chapter. "Subsidies" refers to the benefits that exporters derived from various export promotion measures.

The authors' estimation of "subsidies" takes into account such export promotion measures as direct subsidies, internal tax exemptions, tariff exemptions, and interest rate subsidies on export credit. Thus, some export promotion measures were left unaccounted for: priority in credit allocation that exporters enjoyed under the export credit system, the implicit encouragement of export in the trader registration system, and the assistance provided by KOTRA. However, these measures did not directly affect individual exporters' earnings, and their impact on export must also have been indirect.

Thus estimated, the "effective exchange rate on exports" represents exporter earnings in current won for a current dollar's-worth of export. The authors then translate this into real terms by dividing the estimates by Korea's wholesale price index and multiplying it by major trader partners' wholesale price index to get the "purchasing-power-parity effective exchange rate on exports", which represents exporters' earnings in constant Korean won for a constant dollar's-worth of exports. Figure 2.3 shows the estimated earnings in indices with 1965 as the base year.

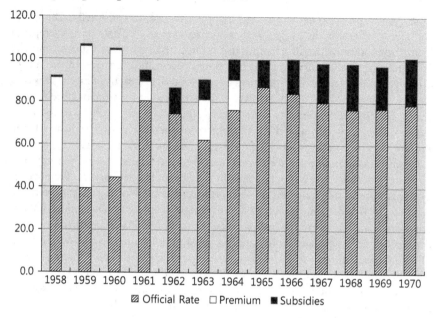

Figure 2.3 Earnings per dollar exports, index, 1958–1970 (1965 = 100).

Note: Frank, Kim, and Westphal (1975), Table 5.8, pp. 70–71, estimate "purchasing-power-parity effective exchange rates on exports", which represents exporters' earnings per dollar exports in Korean won in real terms. I have turned these "exchange rates" that the authors estimate into indices with 1965 as the base year. This figure graphically presents the indices.

Anyone expecting to find the cause of the beginning of rapid export expansion in exporters' earnings would be disappointed. As Figure 2.3 plainly shows, there was no big jump in the earnings that might have had triggered the beginning of the export "explosion". On the contrary, earnings in real terms were declining in 1961, when the rapid export expansion suddenly began. Moreover, "subsidies" had made up less than 5 percent of exporters' earnings before and during 1961. Surely, the changes in exporters' earnings (and hence the export promotion measures taken by the government up to 1961) cannot have been the cause of the rapid export expansion.

2.2.3 Foreign exchange reform in February 1961

In February 1961 the newly elected Chang Myon government carried out a major reform of the foreign exchange system. The reform had been a campaign pledge of the Democratic Party, of which Chang Myon was the head, in the election held in July 1960 to replace the Syngman Rhee government, which had been ousted by the student revolution in April. For years the Democratic Party had labeled the unrealistically low official exchange rate a "disguised subsidy" provided by those in power to their cronies. For instance, if a politician, by exercising some influence on the relevant ministry, had a certain amount of government-held dollars allocated to his political supporter(s) at the official exchange rate, which was always far below the ongoing market rate, it certainly would be an egregious example of corruption. The Democratic Party promised to eradicate this source of widespread corruption should it seize power.

The reform of the foreign exchange system in February 1961 comprised of two main parts. One was devaluation of the won, the Korean currency. As was discussed in the previous chapter, on the occasion of resuming economic cooperation between Korea and the US—relations that had been temporarily discontinued at the time of the student revolution in April 1960—the US government demanded devaluation. The new Korean government readily agreed to it and raised the exchange rate from 65 won to the dollar to 100 won to the dollar on January 1, 1961. The next month, the government once again devalued won on its own initiative by raising the exchange rate to 130 won to the dollar as part of the major reform.

The other main part was the abolition of multiple exchange rates and the adoption of a fixed, uniform exchange rate. For the purpose, the "foreign exchange deposit system" was replaced by a "foreign exchange buying system". As was discussed in the previous chapter, under the old system the traders had held foreign currency-denominated accounts with the Bank of Korea and bought and sold foreign exchanges by transferring the balance in their accounts to the accounts of others. This had given rise to "transfer rates". Under the new system the traders who earned foreign exchanges had to surrender them to the Bank of Korea at the new official rate and were issued certificates valid for 90 days, which entitled the holder to buy back the foreign exchanges. Though illegal, the certificates were traded in the curb market, giving rise to "certificate rates". This system was in effect until June 1961, when the new military government that had come to power in the previous month, May, began to crack down on the curb market.

Table 2.3 shows the extent of the overvaluation of the Korean won in the 1950s and 1960s and the effect of devaluations. The "Market/Official" ratio represents the ratio of "transfer rates" to the official exchange rate for 1955–1961 and the ratio of "certificate rates" to the official exchange rate for 1963–1964. The ratio is not shown for 1962 as the market transaction of the certificate was not allowed, as noted above. The ratio reappears in 1963 and 1964, as the new government instituted a full-scale export–import link system, under which import rights gave rise to a premium on export dollars. This was a response to the worsening trade deficit and sharply declining foreign exchange holdings in those years. As supplementary information, an alternative indicator of won overvaluation for all years from 1955 to 1970 is shown in the table, namely, the "Curb Market/Official" ratio, which is the ratio of the curb market exchange rate of US greenbacks to the official exchange rate. Both ratios, when equal

Table 2.3 Extent of won overvaluation

	Exchange rates			Ratio (Market /Official)	Ratio (Curb Market/ Official)
	Market	*Official*	*Curb market*		
	(1)	*(2)*	*(3)*	*(4) = (1)/(2)*	*(5) = (3)/(2)*
1955	79.0	30.3	77.6	2.61	2.56
1956	102.8	50.0	96.6	2.06	1.93
1957	109.0	50.0	103.3	2.18	2.07
1958	114.6	50.0	118.1	2.29	2.36
1959	134.6	50.0	125.5	2.69	2.51
1960	158.1	62.8	143.7	2.52	2.29
1961	147.0	127.4	148.3	1.15	1.16
1962	NT	130.0	134.0	n.a.	1.03
1963	169.8	130.0	174.5	1.31	1.34
1964	254.0	214.3	285.6	1.19	1.33
1965	NT	265.4	316.0	n.a.	n.a.
1966	NT	271.5	302.7	n.a.	1.11
1967	NT	270.7	301.8	n.a.	1.11
1968	NT	274.6	304.1	n.a.	1.11
1969	NT	285.3	323.6	n.a.	1.13
1970	NT	304.5	342.8	n.a.	1.13

Source: Frank, Kim, and Westphal (1975), Table 3.1, pp. 30–31.

Notes: I estimated the "market" rate on the basis of transfer rates for 1955–1961 from the source. It is a weighted average of the transfer rate on "Japan export dollars" and that on "Other export dollars", the weights being the proportions of the respective exports to two destinations in total exports. For 1963 and 1964 the market rate represents the certificate rate. The annual average of the market rate was estimated by taking into account the number of days the market rates were in effect. I estimated the annual averages of curb market rates for 1955, 1960, 1961, 1964, and 1965 by taking into account the number of days the rate was in effect. The averages of the official exchange rate for 1964 and 1965 and the premium on export dollars in 1965 are taken from Frank, Kim, and Westphal (1975), Table 8.10D, appendix to Chapter 8. n.a. = not available; NT = no transaction.

to 1, indicate no overvaluation of won; the further the ratio climbs above 1, the more overvalued was the won. Interestingly, both ratios show a remarkably similar trend.

The effect of the foreign exchange reform in February 1961 on won over-valuation was drastic, as Table 2.3 shows. In the second half of the 1950s the annual average of the Market/Official ratio was around 2.6 at times, and always greater than 2.0. In 1961, as the result of the reform, the market rate was only slightly higher than the official rate, by around 15 percent. Thus, the reform nearly eliminated the won overvaluation that had been the rule throughout the 1950s. The won became overvalued again in 1963 and 1964, as the official exchange rate fell below the market rate, i.e., the "certificate rate", because of the re-institution of the full-scale export–import link system mentioned above.[8]

However, the won overvaluation lessened in the subsequent years, as the Curb Market/Official ratio indicates.

The other drastic change brought about by the reform was the abolition of multiple exchange rates. This point may be appreciated by recalling the IMF consultation report that provides the following snapshot of the complex exchange rate structure in January 1961, one month before the reform:[9]

> Prior to the exchange reform in February 1961 Korea operated a complicated multiple-rate system which comprised principally an official rate, auction rates for ICA (International Cooperation Administration) financed commodities and for exchange sold by the government for imports, and various kinds of transfer rates in the free market depending on the original sources of exchange, i.e., bilateral account dollars (from exports to Japan), other areas' export dollars (from exports to other areas), military supply dollars (supply of goods to UN forces), military service dollars (supply of services to UN forces), missionary dollars (remittances received by missionaries). Aid-financed imports were programmed by commodity. Imports eligible to be financed with auctioned government exchange were announced by the government for each auction.

Moreover, except for the official rate, these rates were all fluctuating. The auction rates for the aid dollars averaged 99.74 won to the dollar in 1960 and 128.9 won to the dollar in January 1961, while the other auction rates for the dollars held by the Korean government averaged 105.84 won to the dollar in 1960 and 125.5 won to the dollar in January 1961. The average transfer rate in 1960 was 142.0 won to the dollar for Korean–Japanese bilateral account dollars, and 128.0 won to the dollar for other-area dollars.[10]

2.3 How the rapid export expansion began

The reform of the foreign exchange system in February 1961 made the system very simple: now there existed only one, realistic exchange rate. The unusual phenomenon discussed in the section "The beginning of rapid export expansion" above followed: new export items appeared and their exports grew very rapidly, incomparably faster than the exports of existing items, which grew at a "snail's pace". This bifurcation of export items can be readily explained if the reform suddenly and greatly boosted the profitability of export for the new items, while leaving it little changed for the existing export items. But, of course, this was not the case: the same, realistic exchange rate applied to all exports.

Nevertheless, it is a possibility that the same reform represented different things to different people. Indeed, to those who were currently in the export business, the reform meant no change as far as their export earnings were concerned. Before the reform, under the foreign exchange deposit system they kept their export proceeds in the accounts they held with the Bank of Korea, as was discussed in the previous chapter, and all along they had been selling the dollars at the transfer rates, namely, the market rates that the new official rate approximated at the time of the reform. That is, the exchange rate changed little for them. Also, they must have enjoyed the benefits derivable from various export promotion measures that had been in effect. Thus, their export earnings in won were little affected by the reform, and it is reasonable to assume that the exporters had been maximizing profits as hard before the reform as they were after the reform. Therefore, there was nothing that would have them drastically change their export behaviors. The increase in their exports of the 1960s must have been the exporters' response to changes in policies and circumstances other than the reform, and not the reform itself.

On the other hand, for those who had not been in the export business, the reform could have been an eye-opener to profitable export opportunities. In the late 1950s the export business simply was not important enough to most Koreans; total exports amounted to less than 1 percent of GNP, and export sales accounted for merely 2.5 percent of the manufacturing sector's gross output. It may not even have occurred to most businesspeople that they could export their products. Even if one were interested in the possibility, the very complicated structure of foreign exchange rates must have made it difficult to find out if a profitable opportunity existed. It would have required an expert to know what was going on in the foreign exchange markets, and which of the many exchange rates to use for price comparison between domestic and foreign markets. Under the circumstances, it is hardly surprising that someone who may well soon export their products in subsequent years had not yet recognized the export opportunity that they had been sitting on.

Then, by doing away with the multiple exchange rates and adopting a uniform and realistic exchange rate, the reform made international price comparison simple. It now became obvious for Korean businesspeople, as well as for foreign buyers, whether profit could be made by exporting an item at the uniform exchange rate. In addition, a change in banking practice that began the following year must have helped. The Bank of Korea, the central bank, had been the only bank that could legally handle transactions in foreign exchanges; from April 1962 all five commercial banks began handling foreign exchange transactions. This must have made the exchange rate, now uniform and realistic, a readily available piece of information to anyone who was interested.

In short, it is highly likely that the reform made it possible for those who had not been in the export business to see for the first time the profitable export opportunities that had lain hidden behind the veil of a complex and distorted foreign exchange system. Korea in the early 1960s, with little accumulated capital, a science and technology level far behind other countries, and no remarkable natural resources, undoubtedly had a comparative advantage in labor-intensive manufactures—labor being the only factor of production it had in abundance. However, the export of labor-intensive manufactures had been almost nil until 1961: the country's comparative advantage had been virtually unexploited.[11]

Therefore, the export potential of the new items, which were labor-intensive, must have been "unlimited" in the early 1960s. For these reasons, once it had begun, the export of the new items expanded explosively. This account, it seems, well explains the three peculiar features of the rapid export expansion that began in 1961: the appearance of new export items of comparative advantage, the explosive export expansion of the new items, and very slow growth of the then-existing export items in comparison.

2.4 Export success and export promotion

The finding in the previous section goes against the widely held view, shared by the early studies mentioned at the outset, that the government's export promotion policy since the mid-1960s started the rapid export expansion. Nor does it support the claim made by the later studies that the industrial policy, by remedying the coordination failure that had been blocking Korea's economic growth, led to the investment boom and eventual export surge. Thus, the finding in the previous section calls for a re-examination of the causal relationship between Korea's export success and its government policies.

First of all, it is clear that the export promotion policy could not have started the rapid export expansion. It is a fact that the main pillar of the government's development policy had been industrialization through import substitution, and it changed to export promotion in the mid-1960s. The export promotion policy could not have started the rapid export expansion that began in 1961. Rather, evidence suggests that the adoption of the export promotion policy was inspired by the beginning of the rapid export expansion. An example of such evidence can be found in the *First Five-Year Economic Development Plan for 1962–1966* that the Korean government adopted in 1961 and revised in 1964. While the original Plan mentions the desirability of and some policy measures for export expansion, it explicitly states that the policy's priority was import substitution.[12] Obviously, the Plan considered export promotion a remedial measure to deal with the severe foreign exchange shortage at the time. Neither did the Plan anticipate the dramatic expansion of manufactures exports. It envisaged exports of primary products such as "food products" (SITC 0) and "inedible raw materials" (SITC 2), which had accounted for roughly 80 percent of total exports until 1960, to remain the main items of export and to account for roughly two-thirds of total exports in 1966, the final year of the Plan. Simply put, in 1961 the government did not consider export promotion to be a development strategy.

In the revised Plan announced in February 1964 the export target of "food products" and "inedible raw materials" was adjusted downward. In its place, the target for the combined share of "manufactured goods chiefly classified by materials" (SITC 6) and "miscellaneous manufactures" (SITC 8) was adjusted upward from 16 percent to 38.3 percent of total exports for the final year of the Plan. No doubt this adjustment was made in response to the rapid export expansion of SITC 6+8 from 1961 to the first half of 1963, a period that is known to have been taken into consideration in the revision. More to the point, the revised

Plan emphasizes the promotion of export industries. The section titled "Export Plan" states that export promotion was necessary not just to provide exporters with incentives but to promote the development of export industries. Indeed, the new policy of the revised Plan was to promote labor-intensive manufacturing and handicrafts as export industries and redirect investments away from import-substitution industries to export industries.[13] This revision of the *First Five-Year Economic Development Plan* is clear evidence that the export promotion policy was inspired by the rapid export expansion that had begun earlier.

With hindsight, once rapid export expansion began, the policy shift to export promotion was destined to happen for various reasons. In the early 1960s Korea was in dire need of new sources of foreign exchange, for the US aid that had once financed as much as 80 percent of imports in the 1950s was declining after 1957. The need could be met at least in part by rapid export expansion, albeit from a small base. Also, because it was led by manufactures, export expansion could enable Korea to realize its aspiration for industrialization and growth. In addition, as it was creating new jobs, export expansion was a welcome development for the new power elites, which would enable them to fulfill the revolutionary pledge they had made at the time of the military coup in 1961 that they would save the people from under the poverty line. In short, export expansion was a tailor-made answer to a number of big problems the government had to tackle at the time. It is not at all surprising that the new government grabbed the opportunity and, with such catchphrases as "nation building through export" and "export first", launched all-out efforts for export promotion, to be discussed in the following section.

2.5 Export promotion and its effects

Since the mid-1960s the government's export promotion intensified. The government undertook a major devaluation from 130 to 256.5 won to the dollar in May 1964, while dropping direct subsidies and the full-scale export–import link system mentioned above.[14] Instead, it expanded credit incentives by increasing the number of types and the volume of preferential loans for export.[15] In June the government announced the "Comprehensive Export Promotion Program". Referring to the export promotion measures until then as "piecemeal and improvising" in nature, the Program attempted to provide the export promotion with a comprehensive and consistent framework and extended the policy supports to export production as well as export.[16] The Program also intended to pick industries for promotion, help small and medium-sized firms turn into exporters, provide industrial parks for export production, expedite the import of capital equipment for export production, secure raw materials for export production, and so on.

In 1965 export promotion was further strengthened. The financial reform of the same year raised ordinary bank loan rates from 16 to 26 percent, but the preferential loan rates for exporters were kept unchanged at 6.5 percent and were subsequently lowered further.[17] In the same year a "wastage allowances" scheme, specified by export items, was introduced, which generously set the limit of tariff exemption for imported intermediate inputs for export production over and above established needs. Since this was applied to goods and raw materials, the import of which was limited or subject to high duties, exporters could sell the unused portion in the domestic market for profit. Also, in order to encourage the use of domestically produced intermediate goods in exports production, a system of local "letters of credit" (L/Cs) was introduced. This allowed exporters to issue local L/Cs, on the basis of original L/Cs they received, to domestic producers of export goods and intermediate inputs, who in turn could issue local L/Cs once again. The domestic producers with local L/Cs enjoyed the same benefits that exporters did concerning preferential loans, import licenses, tax favors, and so on.

Also in 1965 President Park began to preside the monthly "Expanded Meeting for Export Promotion".[18] In the meeting the export performance of the previous month and the progress of the Comprehensive Export Promotion Program were reported, presidential directives were followed up, and so on. Difficulties and problems in export business were also identified, workable solutions were sought and administrative procedures were simplified, and presidential directives were issued. In 1966 tariff exemption was extended to the import of capital equipment for export production as well as intermediate goods and raw materials. Also in 1966, exporters were provided with the benefit of accelerated depreciation for tax purposes.

Clearly, export promotion became the centerpiece of the government's economic policy. As Cole and Lyman (1971) comment: "Briefly, all parts of the Korean Government apparatus that could be of any help were recruited for the export drive."[19] Frank, Kim, and Westphal (1975) observe: "Along with the exchange reform and import liberalization, the period 1964–66 saw marked intensification of export incentives." As was noted at the outset of this chapter, these and other early studies of Korea's economic growth hold the view that the rapid export expansion began during the mid-1960s, when these strong export promotion measures were adopted.[20]

Thanks to the more numerous and stronger export promotion measures, the benefits the exporters enjoyed no doubt became greater in the second half of the 1960s, as Figure 2.3 shows. Was this the reason for Korea's export success, then? The answer is not a simple yes or no, because the export promotion measures were not adopted in a vacuum. As mentioned earlier, the import policy was protectionist under the strategy of industrialization through import substitution, and the government kept the import policy basically unaltered when it was embarking on export promotion. It was only in the early 1980s that import liberalization began in earnest. It should be recalled that protection tends to have an export-depressing effect, as was briefly discussed in the section "Protectionist import policy", above. Thus, in the second half of the 1960s and in the 1970s the government was in effect simultaneously pursuing two policies that had opposite effects on export.

To determine the net effect on export, it is necessary to quantify the effects of these two different policies. Fortunately, this work has already been done by Westphal and Kim (1982) for the year 1968, and the result is briefly described here. The authors first estimate the "effective rate of protection" in the production of export goods, the rate by which the government's trade policy measures increase the value-added in the production over and above the value-added in the hypothetical "free trade" situation of no trade policy measures. Since value-added is the recompense to factors such as labor, capital, and land, which take part in the production, the greater the effective rate of protection, the more encouraged is the production. The trade policy measures, the effects of which were estimated, included the tariffs and quantitative import restrictions that tended to raise the prices of the protected goods in domestic markets and thereby reduce the value-added of export production. Also included were the trade policy measures that exempted the exporters from these import-restrictive measures, as well as such measures as "wastage allowance", mentioned earlier, which provided favors to export production. The authors' estimate of an effective rate of protection for export production in the manufacturing sector is 3.1 percent, with the estimate for all industries at 0.4 percent. That is, the trade policy measures had the effect of slightly increasing the value-added of export production.

Next the authors estimate "effective subsidy rates", which add to the effective rate of protection the effects of such export promotion measures as income tax reduction and preferential loan rates. The effective subsidy rate thus estimated is 12.4 percent for the manufacturing sector and 8.6 percent for all industries. That is, due to the trade policy measures and export promotion measures, the value-added in export production increased by these percentages in manufacturing and in all industries.

Not yet included in the "effective subsidy rates" is the indirect effect of import restriction on export through its effect on exchange rate; import restriction reduces the demand for foreign exchange and, therefore, lowers the exchange rate. The consequence is a reduction of the value-added in Korean won for the producer. The authors estimated that the import-restricting policy measures lowered the won–dollar exchange rate by 9.1 percent, that is, the value-added in won in export production declined that much because of the import restriction. The rate that adds this negative effect on top of the effective subsidy rate is called "net effective subsidy rate", and the authors estimate the rate to be –0.3 percent for export production in the manufacturing sector and –3.1 percent for export production in all industries.

In other words, the opposite effects on export of import restriction and export promotion nearly offset each other, and the net effect was a free-trade-like environment for exporters. The estimate was for a single year in the late 1960s. However, it seems certain that the net effect did not become more favorable to export in the following years, for the export promotion measures that had been adopted in the second half of the1960s began to be scaled down in the early 1970s after Korea joined GATT in 1967. For example, the income tax reduction on export earnings was abolished in 1972, and the tariff exemption on imports of raw materials for export production was changed to a tariff rebate system in 1975. The import policy also became a little more restrictive in the 1970s under the "heavy and chemical industry" (HCI) policy (to be discussed in Chapter 4). Therefore, if anything, the net effect of the two different policies may have turned somewhat against export in the 1970s. In short, the export promotion measures the government adopted helped export mainly by neutralizing the negative effects of the protectionist import policy on export, not by providing exorbitantly big favors. Had there been no protectionist import policy, export promotion may not have been necessary.

It needs to be noted that an additional, subtle contribution was made by the export promotion policy, as Krueger pointed out, although it may not have been intended.[21] According to her, the export orientation of the Korean government during the high-growth years made policy mistakes fairly readily apparent, as export performance would be quickly and adversely affected if and when policy mistakes were made. Therefore, "you could not have an export oriented strategy *and* highly unrealistic exchange rate ... very expansionary monetary and fiscal policy ... [emphasis is added]". Thus, export-orientation provided market discipline, as the Korean economy had no choice but to take as given the world market prices. Regardless of whether this "discipline" was intended by the policymakers or not, the contribution may have been substantial.

The export success of the 1960s and 1970s was basically due to the removal of impediments to trade, namely, the complicated foreign exchange system and the negative effects on export of the protectionist import policy. Korea had comparative advantage in labor-intensive manufactures, because the economy was abundant in labor, with a small land mass with no exportable natural resource products, little accumulated capital, and a science and technology level far behind that of other countries. Once the impediments were removed, the economy began realizing its huge export potential, which had been left unexploited until then. Simply put, Korea was exporting those goods of its comparative advantage. However, there was another important fact that should not be forgotten or ignored: in the early 1960s, when Korea's explosive export expansion and rapid industrialization began, the world market was more than 100 times as big as it had been in the 1800s, when European countries were industrializing. This point will be discussed in Chapter 5.

Appendix

Table 2.A1 Exports, 1957–1970 (in thousand dollars)

SITC		1957	1958	1959	1960	1961
0	Food, live animals	3,114	2,456	4,118	9,701	8,948
1	Beverages, tobacco	53	-	106	451	184
2	Crude materials, inedible	14,591	10,583	11,713	15,816	20,598
3	Mineral fuels, etc.	6	297	657	1,147	2,209
4	Animals, vegetable oils	35	162	177	199	118
5	Chemicals	6	10	115	401	550
6	Manufactured goods, classified by materials	3,394	2,408	2,139	3,937	4,004
631211	Veneer sheets	-	-	11	21	1,217
652	Cotton fabrics	276	899	1,425	2,443	857
6532	Woolen fabrics	-	-	-	-	-
6535	Synthetic fabrics	-	-	-	-	-
7	Machinery, transport equipment	56	4	48	88	884
8	Miscellaneous manufactured articles	640	148	86	93	791
83	Travel goods, handbags	-	-	-	-	4
84	Clothing	-	-	-	-	2
85	Footwear	-	-	-	-	30
89941	Umbrellas	-	-	-	-	-
89993	Artificial flowers	-	-	-	-	-
89995	Wigs, false beards	-	-	-	-	-
	Total exports	22,202	16,451	19,812	32,827	40,878

Sources: Bank of Korea, *Economics Statistics Yearbook*, 1960, 1964, 1966; Ministry of Commerce, *Trade Statistics Yearbook*, 1964.

Table 2.A2 Overall index of trade liberalization, 1955–1984 (%)

Year	Average tariffs	Automatic approval	Year	Average tariffs	Automatic approval
1955	27.4	1.0	1970	58.5	52.8
1956	27.4	3.5	1971	57.9	53.5
1957	35.4	6.4	1972	57.5	49.5
1958	42.9	6.3	1973	48.2	50.7
1959	66.5	4.7	1974	48.1	49.3
1960	58.0	5.0	1975	48.1	47.8
1961	36.0	4.0	1976	48.1	49.6
1962	49.6	5.4	1977	41.3	49.9
1963	49.5	0.4	1978	41.3	61.3
1964	51.0	2.0	1979	34.4	69.1
1965	52.7	5.9	1980	34.4	70.1
1966	52.3	9.1	1981	34.4	75.5
1967	52.6	58.8	1982	34.4	77.4
1968	58.9	56.0	1983	34.4	81.2
1969	58.3	53.6	1984	26.7	85.4

Source: Kim (1991), Table 3.6.

Note: Automatic-approval (AA) items are shown as a percentage of total importable items.

1962	1963	1964	1965	1966	1967	1968	1969	1970
21,847	16,506	26,350	28,190	40,478	37,928	44,491	50,279	65,537
14	250	184	897	6,892	7,019	8,621	14,850	14,231
19,372	27,742	31,441	37,033	46,679	58,005	61,506	73,042	99,973
2,760	2,579	2,488	1,899	1,505	1,772	2,298	4,837	8,761
69	92	88	71	137	119	113	68	59
990	904	630	380	714	2,359	3,115	9,753	11,413
6,177	28,115	42,309	66,414	84,175	101,382	143,598	173,826	220,886
2,060	5,833	11,395	18,030	29,880	36,418	65,590	79,162	91,746
1,834	4,289	11,119	10,522	10,121	12,591	13,314	18,645	26,355
-	10	580	2,228	2,153	3,963	4,519	3,344	3,382
2	471	1,040	2,507	4,402	9,853	16,653	12,646	9,962
446	4,066	2,204	5,501	9,556	14,185	24,464	53,219	61,469
1,954	6,400	13,198	34,487	59,197	97,238	167,005	242,344	352,496
1	2	6	50	417	1,209	827	1,228	2,479
1,119	4,644	6,614	20,713	33,385	59,208	112,232	160,770	213,566
238	738	879	4,151	5,467	8,139	11,044	10,476	17,268
1	-	72	86	26	50	203	431	799
37	107	319	511	423	397	727	599	881
-	13	169	2,344	12,022	22,724	35,092	60,199	100,868
54,813	86,800	119,057	175,081	249,537	320,227	455,397	622,513	835,182

Notes

1 This chapter heavily draws upon Yoo (2017).
2 One of the earliest studies was Cole and Lyman (1971), especially chapter 8, "The Patterns of Economic Policy". In addition, there were Frank, Kim, and Westphal (1975), Kim (1975), Hong and Krueger (1975), Kim and Westphal (1976), and Krueger (1979), among others.
3 See, for example, Rodrik (1995).
4 Import substitution under protection was the standard policy for industrialization recommended by the economics profession in the 1950s and 1960s. It was after the East Asian experience that the benefits of an open trade regime began to be recognized by the profession. See Krueger (1997).
5 Lerner (1936).
6 Hong (1979), p. 49. See also Frank, Kim, and Westphal (1975), p. 38 and Kim and Westphal (1976), p. 60.
7 Frank, Kim, and Westphal (1975), Table 5.8, pp. 70–71.
8 The rise in premium was in part because the government nearly eliminated all items from the list of automatic-approval (AA) imports in response to the worsening trade deficit. Frank, Kim, and Westphal (1975), p. 47. In May 1964 the government carried out another foreign exchange reform, which included a major devaluation of won.

9 IMF (1961), p. 14.

10 *Ibid.*, Part II, p. 30.

11 According to Frank, Kim, and Westphal (1975), pp. 96–98, the norm for exports share in GDP across countries of comparable population and per-capita income in 1955 was 9.8 percent of GDP for large countries and 8.1 percent for large manufacturing countries, while the actual share for Korea in 1955 was 1.7 percent. The "exports" here seem to include services as well as goods. According to Hong (1979), exports were as large as 31 percent of GNP in 1940, although it is debatable whether all of them should be regarded as international trade, as most of them went to Japan.

12 Economic Planning Board (1961), p. 43, clearly states in the section on trade policy that the priority was on increasing the production of the import substitution industries before it mentions various export promotion measures.

13 Economic Planning Board (1964), pp. 44–47.

14 The export–import link system was reintroduced in 1966 with a limited scope to encourage exports with low profit margins and to new markets. See Frank, Kim, and Westphal (1975), p. 51.

15 See Frank, Kim, and Westphal (1975), pp. 49–50. The preferential loan arrangements included loans for suppliers of US offshore procurement (mainly for Vietnam), credits for importers of raw materials and equipment for export industries, export usance (credits for exporters who ship without L/Cs but receive payment after shipment), export industry promotion loans, Medium Industry Bank equipment loans for conversion of factories to export production, Medium Industry Bank equipment loans for specialized export industries.

16 Ministry of Commerce and Industry (1988), especially pp. 222–234.

17 See Table 4.3 in Chapter 4. Also, see Frank, Kim, and Westphal (1975), p. 49:

> The preferential rate on export credits was reduced from 8 percent in 1963 to 6.5 percent in February 1965, and to 6.0 percent in June 1967 ... The Bank of Korea lowered the discount rate on export bills from 4.5 percent to 3.5 percent in 1966. This rediscount of bills was enormously profitable for commercial banks which financed nearly all export credits through rediscounting bills.

18 It was attended by various economic ministers, the governor of the Bank of Korea, the heads of KOTRA, the Korea Traders Association, the Korea Chamber of Commerce, the heads of banks and financial institutions, chairmen of leading export firms, and experts on trade.

19 Cole and Lyman (1971), pp. 190–191.

20 Park (1983) observes that

> Gradually, after joining GATT in 1967 and under pressure from major trading partners, the government moved away from the use of direct incentives in the early seventies, and by 1972 practically all direct incentives had been repealed, revised, or replaced.

21 Krueger (2010).

References

Bank of Korea, 1960, 1964, 1966, *Economics Statistics Yearbook*.

Cole, David C., and Princeton N. Lyman, 1971, *Korean Development: The Interplay of Politics and Economics*, Cambridge, MA: Harvard University Press.

Economic Planning Board, 1961, *The First 5-Year Economic Development Plan 1962–1966*, Seoul: Economic Planning Board (in Korean).

Economic Planning Board, 1964, *The First 5-Year Economic Development Plan, Revised*, Seoul: Economic Planning Board (in Korean).

Frank, Charles R., Jr., Kwang Suk Kim, and Larry E. Westphal, 1975, *Foreign Trade Regimes and Economic Development: South Korea*, New York: National Bureau of Economic Research.

Hong, Wontack, 1979, *Trade, Distortions and Employment Growth in Korea*, Seoul: Korea Development Institute.

Hong, Wontack, and Anne O. Krueger (eds), 1975, *Trade and Development in Korea*, Seoul: Korea Development Institute.

IMF, 1961, "Korea-1960 Consultations", June. www.imf.org.

Kim, Kwang Suk, 1975, "Outward-Looking Industrialization Strategy: The Case of Korea", in Hong, Wontack, and Anne O. Krueger (eds), *Trade and Development in Korea* (pp. 19–45), Seoul: Korea Development Institute.

Kim, Kwang Suk, 1991, "Part I: Korea", in D. Papageorgiou, M. Michaely, and A. M. Choksi (eds), *Liberalizing Foreign Trade* (pp. 1–132), Cambridge, MA: Basil Blackwell.

Kim, Kwang Suk, and Larry E. Westphal, 1976, *Korea's Foreign Exchange and Trade Regimes*, Seoul: Korea Development Institute (in Korean).

Krueger, Anne O., 1979, *The Developmental Role of the Foreign Sector and Aid*, Cambridge, MA: Council on East Asian Studies, Harvard University.

Krueger, Anne O., 1997, "Trade Policy and Economic Development: How We Learn", *American Economic Review*, Vol. 87, No. 1, pp. 1–22.

Krueger, Anne O., 2010, "What Accounts for the Korean Economic Miracle?", paper read at the conference "The Korean Economy: Six Decades of Growth and Development", Seoul, Korea, August 30.

Lerner, Abba P., 1936, "The Symmetry between Import and Export Taxes", *Economica*, Vol. III, No. 11, pp. 306–313.

Ministry of Commerce and Industry, Trade Statistics Yearbook, various issues.

Ministry of Commerce and Industry, 1988, *40 Years of Export Promotion*, Seoul: Ministry of Commerce and Industry (in Korean).

Park, Pil Soo, 1983, "The Incentive Schemes for Export Promotion", presented at the International Forum on Trade Promotion and Industrial Adjustment, Seoul, September 6–15.

Rodrik, Dani, 1995, "Getting Interventions Right: How South Korea and Taiwan Grew Rich", *Economic Policy*, Vol. 10, No. 20, pp. 55–97.

Westphal, Larry E., and Kwang Suk Kim, 1982, "Korea", in Balassa, Bela et al. (eds), *Development Strategies in Semi-Industrial Economies* (pp. 212–279), Baltimore, MD: Johns Hopkins University Press.

Yoo, Jungho, 2017, "Korea's Rapid Export Expansion in the 1960s: How It Began", *KDI Journal of Economic Policy*, Vol. 39, No. 2, pp. 1–23.

3 The transformation of the Korean economy

During the 1960s and 1970s the Korean economy underwent a transformation, which may be likened to that from a caterpillar to a butterfly. At the beginning of the two decades Korea was one of the poorest countries in the world, with an agrarian economy; by the end it was a dynamic, newly industrializing country. This chapter discusses various aspects of this transformation.

3.1 Rapid growth and changes in industrial structure

The growth rate of Korea's GNP jumped to 9.1 percent in 1963, from under 5 percent in the previous years, and remained high in the 1960s and 1970s—as high as 15 percent at times—as shown in Table 3.1. Unexpectedly, the economy registered negative growth in 1980, from which it bounced back the next year, as will be discussed in the next chapter. The average annual growth rate for the 1963–1979 period was 10.1 percent, a growth rate that only a few countries had experienced for an extended period until then. During this period of rapid growth, the components of final demands grew at widely different rates. I divide the final demands into three components—namely, consumption, gross fixed capital formation (excluding inventory changes that tend to be small and without a long-term trend), and exports—and discuss their influence on the economic growth in this chapter.[1]

Table 3.1 shows that, of the three components of final demands, consumption grew slowest at an average annual rate of 8.1 percent for the 1963–1979 period; gross fixed capital formation grew by 19.5 percent on average; growth of exports of goods and non-factor services was fastest, at an average annual rate of 27.8 percent. As a result, the composition of the final demands drastically changed, as shown in Table 3.2. In 1960 almost all of GNP—99 percent—was consumed, while gross fixed capital formation accounted for 11 percent, made possible because of the inflow of foreign aid that financed most of the imports. By 1979 the share of consumption in GNP declined to 73.5 percent, while that of gross fixed capital formation rose to 32.5 percent. Thus, at the end of the 1970s the economy was plowing nearly one-third of its GNP back into capital formation. The share of exports of goods and non-factor services in GNP

Table 3.1 Growth rates of GNP and final demands, 1961–1981 (%)

	GNP	Consumption	Gross fixed capital formation	Exports	Imports
1961	4.8	1.0	4.3	39.1	−6.9
1962	3.5	5.0	20.0	12.1	35.8
1963	9.1	2.2	27.0	7.3	21.0
1964	8.3	4.5	−11.9	40.7	−25.6
1965	7.4	7.7	26.0	52.3	13.1
1966	13.4	7.6	62.0	35.7	57.7
1967	8.9	9.4	21.7	32.7	34.8
1968	12.6	11.6	40.3	41.6	45.9
1969	15.0	10.3	28.3	31.9	24.7
1970	7.9	10.0	1.7	22.9	10.1
1971	9.2	10.4	4.7	20.5	20.4
1972	7.0	6.7	−3.2	40.1	3.6
1973	14.9	7.9	29.2	60.8	35.7
1974	8.0	8.2	7.3	−3.1	16.7
1975	7.1	6.2	9.3	16.6	0.2
1976	15.1	8.8	14.7	43.0	26.9
1977	10.3	7.1	26.6	25.7	23.8
1978	9.7	11.0	39.4	17.5	29.1
1979	6.5	7.6	8.6	−3.8	8.7
1980	−5.2	0.2	−10.6	9.7	−7.3
1981	6.2	3.2	−3.3	17.3	5.3
1963–1979 average	10.1	8.1	19.5	27.8	20.4

Sources: Bank of Korea, *Economic Statistics Yearbook* 1965, 1972, 1975, 1982, 1984.

Notes: The average growth rate for 1963–1979 in each column is a simple average of the growth rates in the respective columns. The latter growth rates were derived by me from the estimates of GNP and the final demands in varying constant prices: 1960 constant won for 1961–1963, 1965 constant won for 1964–1968, 1970 constant won for 1969–1973, 1975 constant won for 1974–1978, 1980 constant won for 1979–1981. Consumption is the sum of private and government consumption. Gross fixed capital formation is the sum of private and government capital formation and does not include inventory changes. Both exports and imports include trade in non-factor services as well as merchandise trade.

steeply climbed from 3.4 percent in 1960 to around 35 percent in the late 1970s; imports were 12.7 percent as large as GNP in 1960, increasing to 37 percent in 1979. Thus, a Korean economy that had been virtually closed became wide open. By the usual measure of an economy's openness, which expresses in percentage terms the ratio of the sum of exports and imports to GNP, the Korean economy was 6 percent open in 1960, as exports and imports each amounted to roughly 3 percent of GNP, with imports financed by foreign aid excluded; the openness reached nearly 70 percent in the late 1970s.

At the end of the 1970s Korea became a dynamic, newly industrializing economy, led by rapid expansion of foreign trade and capital formation; this capital formation was now mostly financed by domestic saving. In 1979 gross fixed capital formation was 32.5 percent as large as GNP and the current account deficit was 6.7 percent as large. Hence, foreign saving was still financing a sub-stantial part of capital formation, roughly one-fifth. However, unlike in the early 1960s, the inflow of foreign saving in the late 1970s was not foreign aid, but mostly commercial foreign borrowing, as will be discussed below. The increase in domestic saving that supported capital formation was, of course, the other side of the big drop in consumption as a proportion of GNP during the 1960s and 1970s, which largely reflected the drop in the percentage share of private consumption in the GNP. The proportion of the government's consumption declined somewhat but not as much, as Table 3.2 shows.

Korea's industrial structure also underwent remarkable changes. Table 3.3 divides the economy into three main sectors, "primary", "manufacturing", and

Table 3.2 Composition of final demands (%)

	Consumption	Private	Government	Gross fixed capital formation	Exports	Imports(-)	Sum
1960	99.2	84.7	14.5	10.8	3.4	12.7	100.70
1970	82.7	72.3	10.4	24.4	14.2	24.0	97.30
1977	74.9	63.2	11.7	26.0	35.1	35.1	100.90
1979	73.5	62.3	11.2	32.5	30.3	37.0	99.30

Source: Table 3.A1.

Notes: The composition in this table is based on GNP estimates in current prices. Included in exports and imports are trade in non-factor services as well as merchandise. The sum of the shares is not exactly equal to 100 percent, as inventory change is not included and also due to statistical discrepancy.

Table 3.3 Changes in industrial structure

	Primary sector	Agriculture, forestry, and fisheries	Manufacturing	Other
Sector shares in GNP (%)				
1963	44.8	43.1	14.5	40.7
1970	28.3	26.8	20.8	50.9
1977	24.4	23.0	27.0	48.6
1979	21.6	20.5	26.9	51.5
Sector shares in employment (%)				
1963	63.9	63.2	7.9	28.1
1970	51.6	50.4	13.2	35.2
1977	42.6	41.8	21.6	35.8
1979	36.6	35.8	22.9	40.5

Sources: Bank of Korea, *Economic Statistics Yearbook* 1972, 1980, 1983.

Notes: The three sectors' shares in GNP are based on the estimates in current prices of GNP originating from the sectors. The earliest date for which the employment statistics by sectors are available is 1963.

"other", representing the rest of the economy, and shows the shares of GNP originating from the three sectors for selected years from 1963 to 1979. The table also shows the share of the labor force employed in each sector. In 1963 the primary sector's contribution to GNP was 45 percent, employing 64 percent of all workers. By 1979 the sector's contribution to GNP had shrunk to 22 percent and its employment share to 37 percent. The primary sector's contribution shrank, although the agricultural industries' value-added grew on average at a respectable rate of 4.2 percent in real terms (not shown in the table) during the period, as the other two sectors grew much faster.

The manufacturing sector greatly expanded. The share of GNP originating from the sector nearly doubled from 14.5 percent in 1963 to 27 percent in 1979, while the employment share nearly tripled from 8 percent in 1963 to 23 percent in 1979. The growth of the manufacturing sector continued in the next decade, but at a much slower pace. During 1963–1979, the rest of the economy—namely, the sector labeled "other"—increased in relative importance but not as rapidly as the manufacturing sector. The share of the "other" sector in GNP rose from 41 percent to 51.5 percent, while its share of employment increased from 28 percent to 40.5 percent.

3.2 The driving force

The main driving force of the transformation was export expansion. This section discusses the influence of export expansion on the economy by utilizing the input-output tables published by the Bank of Korea.[2] The tables divide the whole economic activity into a number of "industries" and for each industry—say, Industry A—show how much of A's outputs were produced in a given year to meet the final demands for its own products *and* to meet other industries' demands for A's products. Other industries may need A's products as intermediate inputs in their production to meet the final demands for their own products. Thus, the input-output table makes it possible to trace the amount of outputs an industry produces to meet, directly and indirectly, each of the three different components of final demands. Taking export as an example, an industry's outputs may be directly exported and also indirectly exported, as its outputs are used by other industries in producing their own products that are exported. An industry's outputs that are directly and indirectly exported may be called the industry's "gross outputs" for export; the economy's gross outputs for export are simply the sum across all industries of their gross outputs for export. Likewise, the economy's gross outputs for consumption and for gross fixed capital formation can be traced by utilizing the input-output tables.

For those years for which the input-output tables are available, Table 3.4 shows the economy's total gross outputs and the percentage shares of total gross outputs that were produced to meet, directly and indirectly, the three components of final demands: consumption, gross fixed capital formation, and exports. The total gross outputs grew at an average annual rate of 12.3 percent in real terms from 1963 to 1978 and multiplied 5.7 times, faster than the growth

Table 3.4 Total gross outputs and final demands, selected years

	Total gross outputs (billion 1975 won)	Consumption (%)	Gross fixed capital formation (%)	Exports (%)
1963	5,320.40	86.2	9.4	4.4
1966	7,212.30	74.5	14.7	10.8
1968	8,868.50	69.7	17.8	12.5
1970	11,697.40	66.8	20.3	12.9
1973	16,093.50	58.2	15.7	26.1
1975	20,605.80	57.8	16.9	25.3
1978	30,115.30	53.9	19.7	26.4
Growth rate (%), 1963–1978	12.3	8.8	17.9	26.5

Notes: Total gross outputs in 1975 constant won are estimated in Table 3.A3. The percentages of gross outputs that are produced to meet the three components of final demands are calculated from the input-output tables for the years in the 1960s and simply read off the tables for the years in the 1970s. The last row shows the growth rates in real terms of the economy's total gross outputs and of the gross outputs for the three components of the final demands.

of real GNP, which was on average roughly 10 percent for the same period. In 1963, of the economy's total gross outputs, 86 percent were produced for consumption, 9 percent for gross fixed capital formation, and a meager 4 percent for exports. These percentage shares underwent drastic changes. In 1978, of the total gross outputs, 54 percent was for consumption, 20 percent for gross fixed capital formation, and 26 percent for exports. Of course, the reason for the change in relative importance was that the gross outputs for final demands grew at different rates: the gross outputs for exports grew at an average annual rate of 27 percent, and gross outputs for capital formation and consumption at 18 and 9 percent, respectively.

Table 3.5 divides the economy into the primary sector, the manufacturing sector, and the "other" sector, and shows for each sector what Table 3.4 shows for the entire economy. This helps one to see what went on behind the changes in the industrial structure, shown in Table 3.3. As expected, the changes in the industrial structure were largely determined by the export demand. For example, growth of the manufacturing sector's gross outputs was the most rapid, at an average annual rate of 16 percent during the 1963–1978 period, with gross outputs multiplying 9.2 times. This was mainly due to the fact that the proportion of exports as a source of demands for the manufacturing sector's outputs was the largest among the three sectors and the export demand increased most rapidly among the three sectors, at an average of 31 percent per annum. The proportion of exports as a source of demands for the sector's outputs increased from 6.7 to 40 percent. The demand for the sector's outputs for gross fixed capital formation also grew at a rapid average rate of around 20 percent per annum. On the other hand, the importance of consumption as a

Table 3.5 Gross outputs and final demands by sector, selected years

	Primary (billion 1975 won)	Consumption (%)	Gross fixed capital formation (%)	Exports (%)
1963	1,553	95.6	1.5	2.9
1966	2,117	91.6	2.2	6.2
1968	2,132	90.4	2.9	6.8
1970	2,291	87.1	5.5	7.4
1973	2,562	85.0	3.6	11.5
1975	3,120	84.7	3.7	11.6
1978	4,271	86.1	4.1	9.7
Growth rate (%), 1963–1978	7.0	6.2	14.3	16.0

	Manufacturing (billion 1975 won)	Consumption (%)	Gross fixed capital formation (%)	Exports (%)
1963	1,530	82.1	11.2	6.7
1966	2,441	69.0	15.3	15.7
1968	3,221	64.8	17.6	17.6
1970	4,145	59.8	19.1	21.0
1973	6,815	46.4	13.1	40.6
1975	9,742	47.5	15.0	37.6
1978	14,120	42.4	17.6	39.9
Growth rate (%), 1963–1978	16.0	11.0	19.5	30.6

	Other (billion 1975 won)	Consumption (%)	Gross fixed capital formation (%)	Exports (%)
1963	2,737	82.5	13.6	3.8
1966	2,163	66.0	24.0	10.0
1968	3,516	61.8	26.9	11.3
1970	5,261	63.4	27.6	9.0
1973	6,717	60.0	23.0	17.1
1975	7,743	60.0	24.8	15.2
1978	11,725	56.0	27.9	16.1
Growth rate (%), 1963–1978	13.6	10.7	19.1	25.0

Note: The percentage shares of each sector's gross outputs to meet the three components of final demands are based on current price estimates of the gross outputs in the input-output tables.

source of demand for the sector's gross output was almost halved from 82 percent to 42 percent.

In contrast, the primary sector's gross outputs grew slowest, at an average annual rate of 7 percent, multiplying 2.8 times in the 1963–1978 period. As a source of demands for the sector's outputs the primary sector's export demands were the lowest among the three sectors and export demands also grew slowest, at an average annual rate of 16 percent for the period. Its dependence on consumption was the highest among the three sectors, and its consumption demands grew slowly at 6.2 percent on average during the period. The "other" sector's gross outputs grew at an average annual rate of 14 percent from 1963 to 1978 and multiplied roughly 4.3 times, faster than the output growth of the primary sector but slower than that of the manufacturing sector. This was due to the fact that the demand for the sector's gross outputs for exports grew by an average annual rate of 25 percent during the period, faster than the export demand for the primary sector's outputs but slower than that for the manufacturing sector's outputs. Thus, the dependence of the "other" sector on export demand for gross output increased from 4 to 16 percent. During the same period the sector's dependence on consumption demand for its output declined from 82.5 to 56 percent, while the dependence on fixed capital formation increased from 14 to 28 percent. This sector's dependence on the demand of gross fixed capital formation for its outputs in the late 1970s was much higher than the other two sectors' dependence on gross fixed capital formation.

As has been discussed, export also had the most powerful influence on the growth of economic activities at the sector level. It should be noted, however, that what has been discussed so far is only part of the influence that export had. According to Table 3.4, of the economy's total gross outputs 26.4 percent was produced to meet the export demands in 1978. While this was significant, it was not the only influence. In addition, export must have had an indirect influence on the economy, as it affected the other components, namely, consumption and fixed capital formation. Needless to say, if not for exports, GDP would have been much smaller, and consumption expenditure would have been much smaller. Likewise, fixed capital formation must have been much greater than what it would have been without exports, since rapid export expansion undoubtedly created profitable business opportunities. To estimate *how much* greater is beyond the scope of this book. Nevertheless, it is certain that Tables 3.4 and 3.5 show only part of the influence that export had on the growth of the economy. To say, based on the tables, that the consequence of zero export on the economy in 1978 would have been just 26.4 percent smaller gross outputs is a gross understatement.

Moreover, there is still another kind of "gains from trade" due to expanding export (indeed, expanding trade), which cannot be read from Tables 3.4 or 3.5. The changes in the industrial structure brought about by expanding exports, to the extent that they reflect entrepreneurs' decisions, necessarily imply that the economy's resources were better utilized as a consequence, because it may be safely assumed that entrepreneurs allocate more of the resources at their disposal to those activities where the return is higher than where the return is lower. The ensuing productivity increase should also be regarded as the gains due to export (and import) expansion.

3.3 Capital accumulation

Capital accumulation, a central feature in the process of economic growth and industrialization, lets a labor-abundant economy become capital-abundant. From 1963 to 1979, while the economy was growing at around 10 percent per annum, gross fixed capital formation grew nearly twice as rapidly, at 19.5 percent per annum, as shown in Table 3.1. This was considerably facilitated by government policies. The new government that came into power in 1961 made efforts to attract foreign capital in the following years and carried out financial reform in the mid-1960s to mobilize domestic financial saving. These policy measures taken at this critical juncture had ramifications, both intended and unintended, that it seems appropriate to note and discuss.

3.3.1 Policies on foreign loans and financial reform

During the 1950s the trade account was always in deficit, and the foreign exchange shortage was severe.[3] As was discussed in Chapter 1, in the second half of the decade the annual trade deficit was around 350 million dollars on average, as the annual exports and imports were on average around 20 million dollars and 370 million dollars, respectively. Foreign aid, which used to finance most of the trade deficit, peaked in 1957 and declined in the following years; it financed 87 percent of imports in 1957 and 39 percent in 1963. Under the circumstances, foreign loans were considered a major policy tool to deal with the foreign exchange shortage, although foreign loans were becoming costly as "soft" loans from public sources declined and "hard" loans from commercial sources increased. Foreign loans were also needed because foreign capital goods were required for a number of projects in the first Five-Year Economic Development Plan for 1962–1966 and in the subsequent Plans.

The "Foreign Capital Inducement Law" had been enacted in 1960, and in July 1962 the government added two procedures to facilitate foreign capital inflow: one to use the export credits of capital goods-exporting countries, the other for granting the government's repayment guarantee on foreign loans. For the repayment guarantee, a foreign loan arranged between Korean borrower(s) and foreign lender(s) had to be approved by the Economic Planning Board, the economic policy-coordinating ministry at the time, and then the Bank of Korea issued the repayment guarantee. Also provided were tax favors such as full or partial exemptions from income tax on foreign lenders' and investors' incomes.

Another policy that strongly affected capital accumulation was the financial reform of September 1965. The reform raised the interest rate on bank deposits, most significantly from 15 percent per annum to 30 percent on the new 18-month time deposits; the rates on ordinary bank loans were also raised, but not by as much. The reform intended to attract domestic financial saving to the banking sector, which had been lent in unregulated financial markets or used to purchase real goods and assets as a hedge against inflation. The inflation rate had been high in the 1950s and 1960s, reaching nearly 30 percent in 1964. Consequently, banks' interest rates on deposits had often been negative in real terms. In contrast, interest rates in unregulated financial markets had been three to four times as high as the ceiling interest rate, which the anti-usury law had set at 15 percent.

The response to the financial reform was dramatic. Time and savings deposits increased by more than 40 percent within three months and then approximately doubled in each of the following three years. Compared to GNP, time and savings deposits were 3.9 percent as large at the end of 1965, and the percentage rose to 32.7 percent at the end of 1969. This is understood as a shift of liquid assets from unregulated financial markets to the regulated financial market, as was intended by the reform, although no estimate is available of the shift. According to Cole and Park (1983), "there was ample evidence at the time that individuals and businesses were adjusting their asset holdings".[4]

The financial reform had an additional consequence that was equally as important: it greatly widened the interest rate gap between Korean banks and foreign banks. This, together with the repayment guarantee of foreign loans introduced in 1962, led to a massive inflow of foreign capital. Foreign debts with maturity of less than three years increased from virtually zero in 1962 to 70 million dollars in 1968, which was nearly 40 percent as large compared to the foreign exchange earnings in the year. In 1966 the government revised the Foreign Capital Inducement Law and limited the repayment guarantee so that the annual debt service arising from such loans may not exceed 9 percent of total annual foreign exchange receipts. The normalization of diplomatic relations between Korea and Japan in 1965 also added to the inflow of foreign capital, as Korea was to receive the Property and Claims Fund from Japan, totaling 500 million dollars in the next ten years.[5]

3.3.2 Becoming a capital-abundant economy

Increases in savings deposits and foreign capital inflow, discussed in the previous subsection, made it possible for gross fixed capital formation to rise from 11 percent of GNP in 1960 to 32.5 percent in 1979, as shown in Table 3.2. In terms of the growth rate, from 1963 to 1979 gross fixed capital formation grew nearly 20 percent per annum in real terms (Table 3.1), while the population was growing at 2 percent per annum. Thus, Korea, once a labor-abundant and capital-poor country, was rapidly becoming a capital-abundant country.

Table 3.6 shows some estimates of gross fixed non-residential capital stock per capita for Korea and three European countries. The estimates for the European countries are reported for selected years from 1820 to 1991 in Maddison (1995) in "1990 Geary Khamis dollars", which is the currency unit designed to reflect purchasing-power parity, according to the author. The estimates for Korea are from Pyo (1998), which reports the non-residential capital stock for 1954–1996 in 1990 constant Korean won. I converted Pyo's estimates into 1990 dollars by applying the won–dollar exchange rate in1990 for all years, as shown in Table 3. A5 in the Appendix to this chapter, and then the results are simply divided by the Korean population for corresponding years to get the estimates of gross fixed non-residential capital stock per capita in 1990 dollars.

The first column of Table 3.6 shows some benchmark figures for the non-residential capital stock per capita: 1,200 dollars, 2,000 dollars, 5,400 dollars, and so on. Each of the other columns shows the estimates for an individual country, which are closest to the benchmark figures and the year for the estimate

Table 3.6 Gross fixed non-residential capital stock per capita, a comparison (1990 constant dollars)

Benchmark figures	Korea	UK	France	Germany
	1,177 (1966)		n.a.	n.a
1,200		1,201 (1820)		
	1,229 (1967)			
2,000	2,004 (1972)			
	3,298(1976)	3,438 (1890)	n.a.	n.a
	4,538 (1978)	4,230 (1913)		
	5,297 (1979)			
5,400				
		5,535 (1950)		
	7,381 (1982)			7,754 (1950)
8,000				
	8,207 (1983)		8,516 (1950)	
10,000	10,166 (1985)			
	15,598 (1989)			
15,700				
		15,792 (1973)		
	19,568 (1991)			
20,000			20,075 (1973)	
25,000	25,028 (1994)			
				25,510 (1973)

Sources: The estimates for Korea are from Table 3.A5, which is based on Pyo (1998), as noted in the text. The estimates for other countries are from Maddison (1995), Table 3a, p. 143.

Notes: The number in the parentheses indicates the year in which the per-capita capital stock is supposed to have reached the estimate. The estimates for other countries are in "Geary Khamis dollars", which, according to Maddison (1995), reflect purchasing-power parity. n.a. = not available.

in parentheses. For example, in the column for Korea the first entry shows that the estimate of per-capita non-residential capital stock that was closest to the benchmark figure of 1,200 dollars was 1,177 dollars for 1966, and the closest to the benchmark figure of 5,400 dollars was 5,297 dollars for 1979.

The table shows that, compared to the advanced economies in Europe, Korea's capital accumulation started very, very late and, once started, proceeded much, much faster. For example, the estimate of the UK's non-residential capital stock per capita for 1820 is 1,201 dollars, slightly greater than 1,177 dollars—the estimate of Korea's for 1966—both in 1990 constant dollars. Thus, in the mid-1960s Korea's per-capita non-residential capital stock was roughly equal to the UK's some 140 years ago. The estimates for the two countries become comparable again around 5,400 dollars: a little less than that for Korea in 1979 and a little greater for the UK in 1950; then the estimates for the two countries become comparable for the third time at around 15,700 dollars: a little less for Korea in 1989 and a little greater for the UK in 1973. Thus, it took the UK 130 years and

Korea 13 years for the per-capita non-residential capital stock to rise from the first comparable level of around 1,200 dollars to the second comparable level of around 5,400 dollars; then it took the UK 23 years and Korea 10 years for the estimates to rise from the second to the third comparable level of around 15,700 dollars. Similarly, France's level of per-capita non-residential capital stock in 1950 was 8,516 dollars, about 4 percent higher than Korea's 8,207 dollars in 1983; France's reached 20,075 in 1973 and Korea's 19,568 dollars in 1991.The rise from around 8,000 dollars to around 20,000 dollars took France 23 years and Korea 8 years. Similarly rapid was Korea's capital accumulation compared to that of Germany.

In sum, in the mid-1960s Korea's capital abundance, represented by the level of non-residential capital stock per capita, was comparable to what it was in Western European countries some 140 years ago. The relative capital abundance rose rapidly in the following two decades. By the early 1990s the per-capita capital stock in Korea was comparable to what it was in Western European countries in the early 1970s, roughly 20 years behind. The Korean economy was rapidly becoming capital-abundant, thanks to the rapid capital accumulation.

3.3.3 The Presidential Emergency Decree of 1972

There was a dark side to this remarkable development: the financial structure of the corporate sector weakened. Most of the fixed capital formation discussed above, roughly 70 percent in the 1960s and 75 percent or more in the 1970s, was made by private firms, who must have been encouraged by rapid export expansion and economic growth. The problem was that, short of equity capital, firms financed the investments by borrowing from all sources. The corporate sector's investments were facilitated by rising deposits in the banking sector, inflow of foreign capital, especially in the second half of the 1960s, as discussed in the section "Rapid growth and changes in industrial structure" above, and were also financed by borrowing from the curb markets (the unregulated financial markets). Thus, the rapid capital accumulation entailed a steep increase in the debt–equity ratio in the corporate balance sheets: the average debt–equity ratio in the manufacturing sector, which was 1.0 in the early 1960s, shot up to 4.0 in 1971.[6] As a result, firms' financial structures became vulnerable to changes in business conditions and interest rates.

A number of unfavorable developments then simultaneously took place within and outside of Korea. The won–dollar exchange rate went up from 271.5 won to the dollar at the end of 1965 to 373.3 at the end of 1971. This, of course, meant a proportionate increase in firms' debt burden in Korean currency for a given amount of foreign borrowing. The world economy had been slowing down since the late 1960s; the US economy in particular, by then Korea's biggest trade partner, was going into a recession in 1970. The growth rate of Korea's total exports in real terms was halved from 42 percent in 1968 to 21 percent in 1971 (Table 3.1). In addition, President Nixon announced a number of measures to defend the dollar in August 1971, including a surcharge 10-percent tariff on all imports. By that time Korean firms' dependence on export had grown substantially after years of rapid export expansion; of the manufacturing sector's total gross outputs, 7 percent was for exports in 1963 compared to 21 percent in 1970 (Table 3.5).

In the early 1970s many Korean firms found themselves in serious financial difficulties, with some going bankrupt.[7] The biggest threat was coming from the curb market. Curb market loans carried high interest rates, and firms could easily go bankrupt if lenders demanded repayment of the loans. In cases where a borrower's risk was deemed high, lenders made such demands or cashed in the promissory note before the due date. Thus, a chain reaction of bankruptcies and ensuing economic chaos were a possibility. If some big firms were to go bankrupt and take subcontracting firms along with them, the lending capability of the banking sector would be impaired, and this in turn could lead to a spread of bankruptcies, as the corporate sector's debt–equity ratio was very high—at 4.0 on average, as noted above. In June 1971 the Federation of Korean Industries (FKI), an organization of big businesses, directly entreated the president to bail the corporate sector out of its financial difficulty.

On August 3, 1972, the president issued an emergency decree that annulled all existing loan contracts between curb market lenders and borrowers, replacing them with new contracts that carried an interest rate of 1.35 percent per month, to be paid back over five years with a grace period of three years. Since, according to a survey by the Bank of Korea, the average loan rate in the curb market in 1971 was 3.84 percent per month, the decree reduced the debt burden of the borrowers to a third of what it had been. Lenders and borrowers were supposed to report the existing loan contracts to a government agency, and curb market lenders were given the option to convert their loans into equity of the borrowing firm. The government had estimated the amount of curb market loans to be somewhere between 60 billion and 100 billion won, and the FKI's estimate was around 180 billion won. The reported amount of total loans turned out to be 345.6 billion won, which was 80 percent as large compared to the total money supply at the time and 58 percent as large compared to the government budget of the year.

The emergency decree was highly successful in the short run. The feared chain reaction of bankruptcies or financial meltdown did not materialize; rather, the growth rate of the economy jumped from 7 percent in 1972 to 14.9 percent the next year. It was not an unqualified success, however, as it had some undesirable long-run consequences. The decree sent a loud and clear message to the business community that the government would bail it out if firms ran into financial difficulties. Obviously, the bigger the firm, the more likely the bailout. This was little different from an implicit insurance against bankruptcy for them. Thus, "too big to fail" became a business credo that had strong and long-lasting influence on corporate behavior. It appears that firms, especially large conglomerates, kept making investments without paying much attention to interest rates. The average rate of return on assets in the corporate sector was always lower than the interest rate they paid throughout the 1970s, 1980s, and 1990s, and the average rate of return on equity capital was often lower than the interest rate in the 1980s and 1990s.[8] The corporate sector's average debt–equity ratio, which had gone up to 4.0 in 1971, stayed up above 3.0 in most of the years until the end of the 1990s. This weak financial structure of large conglomerates was one of the main reasons why a number of them went bankrupt at the time of the Asian currency crisis and why the Korean economy suffered a negative growth of 6.7 percent in 1998.[9]

Appendix

Table 3.A1 Final-demands composition of GNP (%)

	Consumption			Gross fixed capital formation	Exports	Imports (–)	Sum
		Private	Government				
1960	99.2	84.7	14.5	10.8	3.4	12.7	100.70
1961	97.1	83.5	13.6	11.7	5.4	14.9	99.30
1962	96.8	82.8	14.0	13.7	5.0	16.6	98.90
1963	91.3	80.4	10.9	13.5	4.7	15.8	93.70
1964	91.3	82.8	8.5	11.3	5.9	13.5	95.00
1965	92.6	83.3	9.3	14.8	8.5	15.9	100.00
1966	88.2	78.2	10.0	20.2	10.3	20.1	98.60
1967	88.6	78.4	10.2	21.4	11.3	21.8	99.50
1968	84.9	74.5	10.4	25.0	12.6	25.2	97.30
1969	81.2	70.9	10.3	25.8	13.3	25.1	95.20
1970	82.7	72.3	10.4	24.4	14.2	24.0	97.30
1971	84.6	73.9	10.7	22.5	15.7	26.3	96.50
1972	84.3	73.4	10.9	20.6	20.3	25.2	100.00
1973	76.5	67.3	9.2	24.0	30.1	33.2	97.40
1974	79.6	69.4	10.2	25.5	28.2	39.8	93.50
1975	81.4	70.9	10.5	26.0	28.1	36.9	98.60
1976	76.9	65.6	11.3	23.8	32.8	34.6	98.90
1977	74.9	63.2	11.7	26.0	35.1	35.1	100.90
1978	73.6	62.1	11.5	30.7	33.7	36.5	101.50
1979	73.5	62.3	11.2	32.5	30.3	37.0	99.30
1980	80.1	67.1	13.0	32.7	37.7	44.8	105.70
1981	80.4	67.3	13.1	28.5	41.4	45.6	104.70

Sources: Bank of Korea, *Economic Statistics Yearbook* 1980, 1983.

Notes: The composition in this table is based on GNP estimates in current prices. Gross fixed capital formation is equal to total investment less inventory changes. Included in exports and imports are trade in non-factor services as well as merchandise. The sum of the expenditure components is not always equal to 100 percent, as inventory changes are not included and due to statistical discrepancy.

Table 3.A2 Sector shares in GNP (%)

	Primary sector	Agriculture and fisheries	Mining	Manufacturing	Other
1960	38.6	36.5	2.1	14.3	47.1
1961	40.6	38.7	1.9	14.3	45.1
1962	38.6	36.6	2.0	14.3	47.1
1963	44.8	43.1	1.7	14.5	40.7
1964	48.2	46.5	1.7	15.5	36.3
1965	39.6	37.6	2.0	17.9	42.5
1966	36.2	34.4	1.8	18.4	45.4
1967	31.9	30.1	1.8	18.8	49.3
1968	29.8	28.3	1.5	19.8	50.4
1969	29.0	27.6	1.4	20.1	50.9
1970	28.3	26.8	1.5	20.8	50.9
1971	28.4	27.0	1.4	21.0	50.6
1972	27.6	26.4	1.2	22.2	50.2
1973	26.2	25.0	1.2	24.8	49.0
1974	26.0	24.8	1.2	26.1	47.9
1975	26.4	24.9	1.5	26.5	47.1
1976	25.0	23.8	1.2	27.6	47.4
1977	24.4	23.0	1.4	27.0	48.6
1978	23.3	21.9	1.4	27.0	49.7
1979	21.6	20.5	1.1	26.9	51.5
1980	17.7	16.3	1.4	28.8	53.5
1981	19.3	17.9	1.4	29.6	51.1

Sources: Bank of Korea, *Economic Statistics Yearbook* 1980, 1983.

Note: The sector shares are based on the estimates in current prices of GNP originating from the sectors.

Table 3.A3 Estimation of total gross outputs in constant price (billion won)

	GNP		Deflator	Total gross outputs	
	Current prices	1975 constant prices		Current prices	1975 constant prices
	(1)	*(2)*	*(3) = (1)/ (2)*	*(4)*	*(5) = (4)/(3)*
1963	503	3,351	0.150	798.6	5,320.4
1966	1,037	4,378	0.237	1,708.3	7,212.3
1968	1,653	5,196	0.318	2,821.3	8,868.5
1970	2,684	6,363	0.422	4,934.1	11,697.4
1973	5,238	8,463	0.619	9,960.7	16,093.5
1975	9,793	9,793	1.000	20,605.8	20,605.8
1978	22,918	13,877	1.652	49,735.7	30,115.3

Sources: Columns (1) and (2) are from the Bank of Korea, *Economic Statistics Yearbook* 1983. Column (4) figures are from the input-output tables for the designated years, which are available at ecos.bok.or.kr, a website of the Bank of Korea.

Table 3.A4 Gross outputs and final demands, by sector (billion current won)

Year		Consumption	Fixed capital formation	Exports	Gross outputs by sector
1963	Primary	222.8	3.6	6.7	233.1
	Manufacturing	188.6	25.7	15.4	229.7
	Other	277.2	45.8	12.9	335.8
1966	Primary	459.4	11.1	31.1	501.5
	Manufacturing	399.2	88.4	90.5	578.1
	Other	414.7	150.9	63.2	628.8
1968	Primary	612.7	19.5	45.9	678.1
	Manufacturing	663.6	180.8	180.3	1024.7
	Other	690.9	300.8	126.9	1,118.6
1970	Primary	841.5	53.5	71.5	966.5
	Manufacturing	1045.8	334.8	367.9	1748.6
	Other	1407.2	612.4	199.4	2219.1
1973	Primary	1347.2	56.6	181.7	1585.5
	Manufacturing	1955.1	551.4	1711.2	4217.7
	Other	2492.6	955.7	709.2	4157.5
1975	Primary	2642.6	114.2	363.5	3120.3
	Manufacturing	4624.6	1458.2	3659.7	9742.5
	Other	4642.2	1920.2	1180.5	7742.9
1978	Primary	6076.0	290.8	686.2	7053.0
	Manufacturing	9897.9	4111.4	9310.2	23319.5
	Other	10849.8	5400.8	3112.6	19363.2

Notes: This table shows the gross output produced by the three sectors of the economy, namely, primary, manufacturing, and other, to meet directly and indirectly the final demands: consumption, gross fixed capital formation, and exports. For those years of the 1960s, I estimated the gross outputs for each industry by multiplying the corresponding direct and indirect requirement coefficients by the vector of final demands. The result is gross output each industry produced to meet the final demand for all industries' products. Then, the results are summed up for those industries belonging to the primary sector, manufacturing sector, and so on. For example, 222.8 billion won shown above for the row of the primary sector and the column of consumption for 1963 represents the value of output in current prices the industries belonging to the primary sector produced in the year to meet the final consumption demand for all industries' outputs. For those years of the 1970s, the direct and indirect requirements are simply read off the input-output tables.

Table 3.A5 Korea's gross fixed non-residential capital stock, 1963–1995

	Non-residential capital stock (million 1990 dollars)	Population (millions)	Per-capita non-residential capital stock (dollars)
	(1)	(2)	(3) = (1)/(2)
1965	32,048	28.705	1,116
1966	34,285	29.436	1,177
1967	37,029	30.131	1,229
1968	40,798	30.838	1,323
1969	46,447	31.544	1,472
1970	52,572	32.241	1,672
1971	59,650	32.883	1,814
1972	67,157	33.505	2,004
1973	76,913	34.103	2,255
1974	88,448	34.692	2,550
1975	101,365	35.281	2,923
1976	118,224	35.849	3,298
1977	140,412	36.412	3,856
1978	167,783	36.969	4,538
1979	198,835	37.534	5,297
1980	227,810	38.124	5,975
1981	257,699	38.723	6,655
1982	290,272	39.326	7,381
1983	327,539	39.910	8,207
1984	369,396	40.406	9,142
1985	414,840	40.806	10,166
1986	465,018	41.214	11,283
1987	525,569	41.622	12,627
1988	587,655	42.031	13,981
1989	662,121	42.449	15,598
1990	749,825	42.869	17,491
1991	846,657	43.268	19,568
1992	933,379	43.663	21,377
1993	1,012,536	44.056	22,983
1994	1,112,592	44.453	25,028
1995	1,235,138	44.851	27,539

Sources: Column (1): The non-residential capital stock estimated by Pyo (1998) in 1990 constant won is converted into 1990 dollars by utilizing the won–dollar exchange for the year. Column (2): Figures for the Korean population are from the National Statistical Office, *Footsteps of Korea*, 1995.

Notes

1 The final demands usually refer to consumption, investments, government expenditure, and net exports, and investments usually refer to the sum of gross fixed capital formation and inventory changes. In the following discussion inventory changes are not considered, which are usually small and tend to fluctuate from year to year without a trend; government expenditures are not separately considered but are divided into consumption and investment, and each is summed with the private consumption or investments.

2 The input-output tables used are those estimated by the Bank of Korea for 1963, 1966, 1968, 1970, 1973, 1975, and 1978. The tables are available at the Bank's website: ecos.bok.or.kr.
3 Factual information in this subsection is mostly drawn from Frank, Kim, and Westphal (1975) and Cole and Park (1983).
4 Cole and Park (1983), p. 203.
5 Also, the Japanese government was to make 300 million dollars in commercial loans available to Korea. Frank, Kim, and Westphal (1975), p. 106.
6 Krueger and Yoo (2002).
7 Factual information in the rest of this subsection is mostly drawn from Kim (2011), especially chapter 16, "Moratorium on Curb Loans".
8 Joh (1999).
9 In comparison, in the US and Taiwan the average debt–equity ratios for the corporate sector were always lower than 2.0 from the mid-1970s until the end of the 1990s. See Krueger and Yoo (2002).

References

Bank of Korea, 1965, 1972, 1975, 1980, 1982, 1983, 1984, *Economic Statistics Yearbook*, Seoul: The Bank of Korea.
Cole, David C., and Yung Chul Park, 1983, *Financial Development in Korea, 1945–1978*, Cambridge, MA: Council on East Asian Studies, Harvard University.
Frank, Charles R., Jr., Kwang Suk Kim, and Larry E. Westphal, 1975, *Foreign Trade Regimes and Economic Development: South Korea*, New York: National Bureau of Economic Research.
Joh, Sung Wook, 1999, "Profitability of Korean Firms before the 1997 Economic Crisis", *KDI Journal of Economic Policy*, December, Vol. 21, No. 2 (in Korean), pp. 3–54.
Kim, Chung-yum, 2011, *From Hope to Despair: Economic Policymaking in Korea 1945–1979*, Seoul: Korea Development Institute.
Krueger, Anne O., and Jungho Yoo, 2002, "Falling Profitability, Higher Borrowing Costs, and Chaebol Finances during the Korean Crisis", in David T. Coe and Se-Jik, Kim (eds), *Korean Crisis and Recovery* (pp. 157–196), Washington, DC: IMF.
Maddison, Angus, 1995, *Explaining the Economic Performance of Nations: Essays in Time and Space*, Aldershot: Edward Elgar.
Pyo, Hak K., 1998, *Estimates of Fixed Reproducible Tangible Assets in the Republic of Korea, 1954–1996*, Seoul: Korea Institute of Public Finance.

4 Industrial policy in the 1970s

In the early 1970s, when the Korean economy was in the middle of the transformation discussed in the previous chapter, the government embarked on an industrial policy on a grand scale, which aimed at upgrading the industrial structure.[1] On January 12, 1973, at the New Year's press conference, President Park Chung Hee proclaimed that "the government hereby declares the heavy and chemical industry policy that places great emphasis on the measures to promote development of heavy and chemical industries".[2] In June the government published the Heavy and Chemical Industries (HCI) Promotion Plan. For the next six years the government made the utmost efforts to promote the development of six selected industries: iron and steel, non-ferrous metals, electronics, chemicals, general machinery, and shipbuilding. The HCI drive came to an end in April 1979, when the government announced the "Comprehensive Stabilization Program", which intended to restore economic stability by adjusting the speed and amounts of investments in the selected industries. The Program also emphasized greater reliance than heretofore on the market mechanism and conservative management of fiscal policies, among others. The experience with the HCI drive deserves careful examination and evaluation, as it is at the heart of the controversy regarding the proper role of the government in a developing economy.

4.1 Background of the heavy and chemical industry (HCI) policy

Attempts to develop individual heavy and chemical industries had existed before the HCI drive. For example, a law to protect the domestic automobile industry was enacted in 1962, and a machinery industry promotion law in 1967. The Integrated Development Plan of the Petrochemical Industry in 1966 led to the construction of the Ulsan Petrochemical Complex in 1968. Also, the construction of an integrated steel mill began in 1970 and was finished in 1973, becoming the now well-known Pohang Iron and Steel Company (POSCO). However, the HCI policy was different from these earlier efforts in that the government had a particular industrial structure in mind and intended to reshape the manufacturing sector accordingly. For the purpose, the government prepared detailed investment plans at the project level, complete with timetables and locations. Intervention in the economy was heavy and intense, with the main decisions concerning resource allocation in the economy being made by the government. A close observer of the drive put it thus: "The eventual consequence of these efforts was the transformation of a privately led market economy into a government-controlled one, in which the market mechanism was largely replaced by an imperative plan for the promotion of HCI."[3] The HCI policy represents a change of tack in a big way from the export promotion policy of the previous decade.

Why change tack when the export promotion policy was so successful? There were a few reasons. One was a newly arisen security concern. The US had been at war against North Vietnam throughout the 1960s, a situation that was growing less and less popular in America. In 1969 the newly elected President Nixon announced that the US would keep its treaty commitments to its allies, but primarily with air and naval forces rather than with ground forces. Early in 1971 the Nixon administration withdrew the Seventh Division of about 20,000 soldiers from Korea, reducing the number of US ground troops stationed in Korea by a third. This was understood as the beginning of an eventual full withdrawal in the near future, and uncertainty about the nation's security greatly heightened in the minds of Koreans, for a precarious balance in military strength between North Korea and South Korea was thought to have been maintained by the presence of US forces, which was also; perceived as a guarantee of reinforcement of US troops in the event of an attack by the North. This concern about national security played a role in the government's decision to promote development of the heavy and chemical industries, which were expected to serve as the basis of the defense industries.

Another reason for the HCI policy was rising protectionism in advanced industrial countries, which was directed against labor-intensive imports from developing countries. Many protective measures took the guise of punitive action against unfair practices such as dumping and subsidies; some orderly marketing arrangements were made, such as the Arrangements regarding International Trade in Cotton Textiles, or the later Multi-Fiber Arrangement. This rising protectionism was considered a threat to the future of Korea's exports, which were mostly destined to the advanced industrial countries. In addition, there was concern about catch-up by the second-tier newly industrializing countries (NICs) in Southeast Asia, namely, Indonesia, Malaysia, and Thailand. As these countries began to promote exports, following the examples of Korea and other East Asian economies, the possibility could not be ignored that Korea may soon lose its export markets for labor-intensive products to those countries with wage rates lower than Korea's. Potentially more threatening was the prospect that China could become a competitor in the world market, as it had an enormous labor force with wage rates lower still than those of the second-tier NICs. President Nixon visited China early in 1972, and the US and China announced that the two countries would work toward a normalization of diplomatic relations.

Another important development that lent support to the HCI policy was the worsening trade balance, shown in Table 4.1. In the 1960s and 1970s exports were increasing more rapidly than imports, but exports were increasing from a small base, while the dependency of exports on imports was rising. Imports of

Table 4.1 Korea's exports and imports, 1963–1974 (million dollars)

	Trade balance	Exports	Imports	Imports of capital goods	Imports for export production	Import content of exports (%)	Capital goods imports over exports (%)
	(1)	(2)	(3)	(4)	(5)	(6) = (5)/(2)	(7) = (4)/(2)
1963	−474	87	560	116	-	0.0	133.2
1964	−285	119	404	69	7	5.8	58.4
1965	−288	175	463	60	10	5.9	34.3
1966	−466	250	716	172	101	40.4	68.6
1967	−676	320	996	310	135	42.2	96.8
1968	−1,008	455	1,463	533	213	46.8	117.1
1969	−1,201	623	1,824	593	297	47.7	95.3
1970	−1,149	835	1,984	590	386	46.3	70.6
1971	−1,327	1,068	2,394	685	506	47.4	64.2
1972	−898	1,624	2,522	762	688	42.3	46.9
1973	−1,015	3,225	4,240	1,157	1,556	48.2	35.9
1974	−2,391	4,460	6,852	1,849	2,039	45.7	41.4

Source: Economic Planning Board, *Major Statistics of the Korean Economy*, 1983.

intermediate inputs for export production and of capital goods were increasing rapidly. Column (5) of the table represents the Customs Office's estimates of the imports of intermediate inputs for export production, and Column (6) the ratio of these estimates over exports in percentages, which rose from 6 percent in 1964 to nearly 50 percent in the early 1970s. Column (7) shows the ratio of capital goods imports over exports in percentages, which was sometimes around 100 percent.

The widely held view about the worsening trade balance at that time can be read in the reports of the "Evaluation Committee of Professors", a group of well-known professors who every year reviewed the economy's progress under the Five-Year Development Plans and made recommendations to the government.[4] The committee's reports in the late 1960s and early 1970s always expressed grave concern over the increasing trade deficits. Its diagnosis was that the high dependence of exports on imports for intermediate inputs and capital goods was due to Korea's "limping" industrial structure, that is, its relatively well-developed consumer goods industries and backward capital goods industries. On this ground the committee recommended import substitution of intermediate inputs and capital goods. Indeed, there was broad agreement that the solution to the mounting economic problems of the day should be sought in the promotion of the heavy and chemical industries.

4.2 Policy measures for the HCI drive

From the beginning of the HCI drive in June 1973 to April 1979, when the Comprehensive Stabilization Program was announced, the government made the utmost efforts to ensure the drive was a success. It was masterminded by the HCI Promotion Council, which was especially set up in the president's office and headed by the second senior secretary to the president in charge of economic affairs. The government mobilized all conceivable policy measures, as it had for export promotion in the previous decade, this time for the development of selected heavy and chemical industries. It also established new industrial parks and handpicked entrepreneurs for key projects, who had initially been reluctant to participate in the drive because of large investment requirements and uncertain prospects. This section discusses the policy measures adopted by the government for the drive. In the discussion the manufacturing sector is divided for convenience into two groups: the "HC group" and the "light group". The HC group comprises those six industries the HCI policy intended to promote; the light group comprises the rest of the manufacturing industries.

The first policy measure to discuss is tax policy favors. The conditions and legal bases for preferential tax treatment were specified in the special laws that promoted particular industries and the Tax Exemption and Reduction Control Law. This tax law was revised in 1974 to provide the firms belonging to the HC group with tax incentives such as tax holidays, special depreciation of fixed capitals, temporary investment tax credits, etc. The same law was revised again in 1981 after the government stopped the HCI drive in 1979; the revision was essentially a reversal of the previous revision. Figure 4.1 graphically represents the tax favors provided to the HC group during the 1970s, as estimated in Kwack (1985). The author estimated hypothetical "effective tax rates on the marginal return to capital" for the firms under the assumption that they took full advantage of the major incentives provided by the tax system, taking into account the statutory tax rates, various tax incentives, and so on as well as inflation rates.[5]

As the figure shows, after the first revision of the Tax Exemption and Reduction Control Law, those firms in the HC group, if they took full advantage of the tax incentives, could lower the effective tax rate on the marginal return to capital

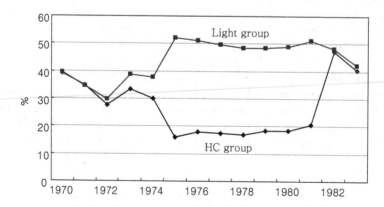

Figure 4.1 Effective corporate tax rate, 1970–1983.
Source: Table 4.A1

from around 30 percent to below 20 percent. On the other hand, the effective tax rate for the firms belonging to the light group was raised from 40 percent to around 50 percent. The figure clearly shows how differently the two groups were treated by the HCI drive. The tax system revamp in 1981 did away with the discrimination.

Import restriction was another policy tool employed by the government for the HCI drive. The trade policy had been on a liberalizing trend since the mid-1960s. In 1967, on the occasion of Korea's joining the General Agreement on Tariffs and Trade (GATT), the regime of quantitative import restriction had shifted from a "positive list system" to a "negative list system". The latter system listed the items that could be imported if prior government approval was obtained; all others were automatically approved (AA) items that could be imported without approval. The proportion of AA items in the total list of importable goods had jumped from 9 percent to 59 percent in 1967, as shown in Figure 2.2 in Chapter 2. However, this liberalizing trend of the import policy was halted or somewhat reversed. The proportion of AA items slightly declined in the early 1970s and dropped below 50 percent in the second half of the 1970s (Figure 2.2 and Table 2.A2, Chapter 2 and its Appendix). This decline in the 1970s was primarily due to increased protection of HC industries, as the products these industries produced were put back on the negative list: mainly chemicals (belonging to SITC 5) and non-electric machinery, electric machinery, and transportation equipment (belonging to SITC 7).[6] Other trade policy measures were also taken, such as reduction of the wastage allowance benefit to exporters, higher investment tax credits to firms purchasing domestically produced machines, and so on.

The most powerful tool of the HCI drive was probably the credit policy called "directed credits" with preferential interest rates. The "directed credits" policy was conducted through the commercial banks, which had been nationalized, and the National Investment Fund that the government created in 1974 to mobilize investable funds. Even before the HCI drive, the government intervened heavily in the commercial banks' credit allocation. As shown in Table 4.2, in the early 1970s the share of policy loans in domestic credit was already large: nearly one-half of the total. During the HCI drive it increased further and accounted for around 60 percent in the late 1970s and early 1980s and then declined to around 50 percent by 1985. Table 4.A2 in the Appendix to this chapter shows that, of the incremental credits that went to the manufacturing sector, those allocated to the heavy and chemical industries used to account for 36 percent in 1973 and 32 percent 1974, and this share jumped to 66 percent in 1975 and remained at around 60 percent in the rest of the 1970s.

Table 4.3 shows the interest rates on ordinary loans, "discounts on commercial bills" in Column (1), two kinds of policy loans, and the inflation rate from 1961 to the early 1980s. During this period, while the loans for exports always enjoyed the lowest interest rate, the interest rate on "loans for machine industry promotion", shown in Column (3), was the next lowest, which is an example of the favored nature of projects of the HCI drive. The interest rate on this loan was

Table 4.2 Share of policy loans in domestic credit (%)

	All policy loans	Foreign trade	Earmarked	Un-earmarked	Incremental ratio	Domestic credit (billion won)
	(1)	(2)	(3)	(4)	(5)	(6)
1970	47.8	5.6	19.4	22.5	n.a.	1,005
1971	48.3	6.1	18.2	24.0	29.1	1,311
1972	53.8	6.7	26.2	20.9	8.3	1,636
1973	55.2	10.5	24.1	20.6	19.8	2,164
1974	53.2	11.2	21.3	20.6	20.6	3,242
1975	53.1	9.0	20.0	24.1	37.4	4,096
1976	52.2	10.0	19.2	23.1	19.1	5,184
1977	55.1	10.4	19.5	25.2	33.0	6,610
1978	60.2	10.8	20.6	28.8	36.4	9,691
1979	58.5	10.6	17.5	30.4	34.3	13,672
1980	59.1	11.5	16.8	30.7	31.7	19,413
1981	58.0	12.7	17.3	28.1	18.2	24,711
1982	53.8	12.3	15.1	26.4	20.3	31,317
1983	53.7	12.7	16.8	24.2	11.8	36,886
1984	52.6	12.7	17.8	22.1	7.7	42,233
1985	51.5	12.9	17.8	20.9	14.4	50,415

Sources: Economic Planning Board, 1986, *Major Economic Indicators*; Bank of Korea, 1986, *Financial System of Our Country*; Ministry of Finance, 1981, *Fiscal and Financial Statistics*; Bank of Korea, *Economic Statistics Yearbook*, various issues.

Notes: Domestic credit includes all loans and discounts to the private sector by the Bank of Korea, deposit money banks, and two development institutions, namely, the Korea Development Bank and the Korea Export Import Bank. "Foreign trade" refers primarily to the loans for exporters by deposit money banks and all loans by the Korea Export Import Bank. "Earmarked" refers to the government funds and the loans for agricultural industries, small and medium-sized firms, and home building. "Un-earmarked" refers to the loans funded by the National Investment Fund, loans in foreign currency, and all loans by the Korea Development Bank. "Incremental ratio" is the ratio of the increment in the "un-earmarked" to the increment in domestic credit, in percentage. n.a. = not available.

much lower than the discount rate charged by commercial banks on commercial bills in Column (1). More to the point, it was lower than the inflation rate shown in Column (4) in all but two years of the 1970s.

4.3 HCI drive and resource allocation

These policy favors of the HCI drive must have affected resource allocation. Table 4.4 shows the facility investments in the manufacturing sector and how much of the investments went to the HC group in the 1970s. The proportion of investments that went to the HC group increased from around 61 percent in 1973 and 1974 to nearly 80 percent toward the end of the decade. While it is very likely that a good part of the increase was the effect of the policy favors, the

Table 4.3 Interest rates and inflation, 1961–1983 (%)

	Discounts on commercial bills	Loans for exports	Loans for machine industry promotion	CPI, percentage change
	(1)	(2)	(3)	(4)
1961	13.9	13.9	n.a.	8.2
1962	13.9	12.7	n.a.	6.6
1963	13.9	9.1	n.a.	20.6
1964	14.0	8.2	n.a.	29.6
1965	16.5	7.6	n.a.	13.5
1966	24.0	6.5	n.a.	12.0
1967	24.0	6.3	n.a.	10.9
1968	24.3	6.0	12.0	11.2
1969	25.2	6.0	12.0	10.0
1970	24.3	6.0	12.0	12.7
1971	22.9	6.0	12.0	13.5
1972	17.7	6.0	10.1	11.5
1973	15.5	6.6	10.0	3.2
1974	15.5	8.9	11.1	24.5
1975	15.3	7.6	12.0	25.2
1976	16.3	7.4	12.4	15.3
1977	16.7	8.0	13.0	10.2
1978	17.8	8.5	14.1	14.5
1979	18.8	9.0	15.0	18.3
1980	24.1	14.8	20.2	28.7
1981	19.4	15.0	17.9	21.3
1982	12.3	10.8	12.1	7.3
1983	10.0	10.0	10.0	3.4

Sources: Bank of Korea, *Economic Statistics Yearbook*, various issues.

Notes: The interest rates shown in this table are weighted averages, weight being the number of months they were in effect in a given year. When the source reports a range that an interest rate took for a year, the midpoint of the range is taken. n.a. = not available.

Table 4.4 Facility investments in the manufacturing sector (billion won)

	All industries	Manufacturing (A)	HC group (B)	Percentage of facility investments in HC group (B/A)
1973–1974	1,054	707	434	61.4
1975	1,098	621	481	77.5
1976	1,279	838	622	74.2
1977	2,026	1,380	1,040	75.4
1978	3,125	2,148	1,719	80.0
1979	3,734	2,469	1,870	75.7

Source: Lee (1991), Table 17.11, p. 452.

Table 4.5 K/L ratios and the changes

K/L ratio (million won per worker, 1980 constant prices)		
	HC group	*Light group*
1966	6.9	3.1
1973	8.2	4.8
1980	15.3	7.0
1985	17.7	9.4
Average annual percentage change in K/L ratio		
1966–1973	2.50	6.45
1973–1980	9.32	5.54
1980–1985	2.96	6.07

Source: Yoo (1990), Table 13, p. 57.

increase may also have been due to other reasons. For one thing, the production technology of the heavy and chemical industries tends to be more capital-intensive, implying that the investment needs are greater in general for the HC group than for the light group.

The effect of policy favors on resource allocation may also be seen in Table 4.5, which shows the capital-to-labor (K/L) ratios, the capital intensities, of the HC and light groups for selected years and the changes in the ratios over time. As expected, the average K/L ratio of the HC group was much higher than that of the light group, often more than twice as high, and the capital intensity was rising in both groups. The effect of policy favors on resource allocation is apparent in the changes in the K/L ratio, which reflect the changes in the costs of capital and labor. Since the "directed credits" policy increased the availability of investable funds and substantially lowered the cost of capital for the HC group, the K/L ratio of the HC group must have increased faster than that of the light group for the duration of the HCI drive. Indeed, that was the case. The average annual growth rate of the HC group's K/L ratio jumped from 2.5 percent in the 1966–1973 period to 9.3 percent in the 1973–1980 period under the HCI drive and went back down to below 3 percent after the drive. In contrast, for the light group the average annual growth rate of the K/L ratio changed in mirror image: it dropped from 6.5 percent before the HCI drive to 5.5 percent during the drive and went back up again to 6.1 percent after the drive.

These contrasting changes in K/L ratios of the HC and light groups were caused by the policy favors under the HCI drive. Tax policy favors to the HC group meant a heightened tax rate for the light group; credit policy favors to the HC group meant less availability and higher cost of credits for the light group; strengthened protection of the HC group meant increased costs of intermediate inputs for the light group. Therefore, investments were diverted away from the light group toward the HC group for the duration of the HCI drive. Therefore, the end of the HCI drive for the light group meant a lower tax burden, lower cost of credits and increased availability of investable funds, and increased profitability. It is not surprising that the end of the HCI drive was immediately followed by an increase in the K/L ratio in the light group.

What was the effect of the HCI policy? The World Bank (1993) examines the effect by asking two questions: first, "did the Korean government's industrial policy bring about an industrial structure that had not been anticipated, given the factor endowments?" Second, "did the policy raise productivity?" On the first question, it finds that despite the government's extensive efforts to promote the development of the heavy and chemical industries, it was the relatively labor-intensive textiles and garments industry that was bigger than international norms predicted in 1988. On the question of productivity change, it finds that

> Although the Korean government selectively promoted chemicals and iron and steel, the large growth in the share of iron and steel was accompanied by quite low TFP (total factor productivity) performance between 1966 and 1985 except for the chemical sector ... On the other hand, textiles and clothing had very high rates of TFP growth.

In sum, "[i]n both cases, our answers lead us to conclude that industrial policies were largely ineffective."[7]

4.4 The impact on the economy

This section investigates the effect of the HCI policy by asking a general equilibrium question: what was the impact on the economy as a whole? The government mobilized all conceivable policy tools for the policy objective and made such important decisions concerning resource allocation in the economy that, as was mentioned in the first section of this chapter, the economy was in a state that may be called "government-controlled". The impact on the economy is hardly expected to be negligible. Indeed, the HCI drive was the main reason for the negative growth of 5.2 percent that the Korean economy experienced in 1980, as will be discussed below.

The Korean economy had been growing at unprecedentedly rapid rates of around 10 percent per year since 1963, and the rate was as high as 15 percent at times in the 1970s, as shown in Table 3.1 in Chapter 3. Based on this experience no one in the mid-1970s would have predicted that the economy would at any point experience negative growth. However, it did. The conventional wisdom, which many subscribe to, attributes the negative growth to three factors. The most often mentioned is the second "oil shock" in 1979, which doubled the international petroleum price and led the world economy into a recession. Another oft-mentioned reason is the "cold summer" in 1980, because of which the agricultural sector's contribution to GNP dropped by 22 percent. The third is the political and social instability that followed the assassination of President Park in October 1979. Thus, the conventional wisdom attributes the negative growth in 1980 to non-economic factors or to events in the world economy

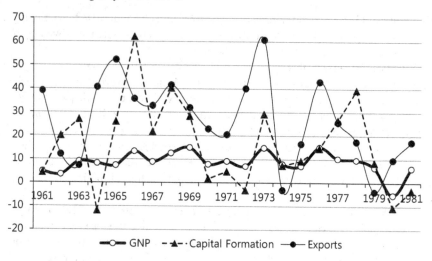

Figure 4.2 Growth rates of GNP, gross fixed capital formation, exports, 1961–1981.
Source: Table 3.1, Chapter 3.

beyond Korea's control. In other words, according to this view, there was basic-ally nothing wrong with the economy.

However, something *was* going seriously wrong with economy. The most important sign was worsening export performance. As shown in Figure 4.2, the annual growth rate of exports in real terms, which was as high as 43 percent in 1976, dropped to 26 and 18 percent in the following two years, and to –4 per-cent in 1979. That is, the export performance had begun to weaken before any of the three events, which the conventional wisdom cites as the reasons for nega-tive growth, took place. The worsening export performance brought investments down, which were closely correlated with exports. As shown in Figure 4.2, the growth rate in investments in real terms dropped from 39 percent in 1978 to 9 percent in 1979, and registered negative growth of –11 and –3 percent in 1980 and 1981, respectively.

It needs to be investigated if and to what extent Korea's poor export per-formance in the late 1970s was due to the external factor of the second oil crisis and/or to some internal factor(s). To investigate the question, Table 4.6 takes a look at two different measures of Korea's market shares in total world exports in the 1970s and the early years of the 1980s. The column titled "World export 1" shows Korea's market share in world exports, unadjusted, which is simply Korea's exports divided by the total world exports, both in current prices. This market share of Korea's exports declined in 1974 at the time of the first oil crisis, when the international petroleum price quadrupled, and again in 1979 and 1980 at the time of the second oil crisis, when the petroleum price doubled. As the petroleum price rose, Korea's market share inevitably shrank, as Korea did not produce or export any petroleum; as the market shares of petroleum-exporting countries

Table 4.6 Korea's market shares in world exports, 1970–1983 (%)

	Korea's market share		Competitors' share in world export 1
	World export 1	*World export 2*	
1970	0.296	0.315	3.682
1971	0.337	0.364	3.970
1972	0.431	0.465	4.257
1973	0.615	0.669	4.327
1974	0.578	0.690	4.101
1975	0.639	0.745	3.935
1976	0.854	1.007	4.493
1977	0.965	1.129	4.435
1978	1.059	1.206	4.658
1979	0.988	1.153	4.898
1980	0.937	1.121	5.183
1981	1.157	1.367	5.474
1982	1.271	1.461	5.540
1983	1.462	1.637	5.776

Source: Yoo (1990), Table 16, p. 92.

Notes: "World export 1" is the sum of all countries' exports. "World export 2" is "World export 1" less OPEC member countries' exports. "Competitors" refer to Hong Kong, Israel, Portugal, Spain, Taiwan, and Yugoslavia.

increased, those of other countries shrank. What needs to be investigated is whether this effect of the petroleum price hike was the only reason for the decline of Korea's market share. The column titled "World export 2" shows an adjusted market share, that is, Korea's exports divided by the world exports total, less the sum of exports of member countries of the Organization of Petroleum Exporting Countries (OPEC). This adjustment shows Korea's share in the world market of non-oil exports. Interestingly, this adjusted market share of Korea's rose in 1974 but declined in 1979 and 1980.

This suggests that the petroleum price hike was not the only reason for the decline in Korea's market share in world exports in 1979 and 1980. It may have in part been due to the weakened competitiveness of Korean exports or, although only a remote possibility, due to a sudden shift in the world demand away from Korea's main export items. In the latter case, too, Korea's market share would decline. To see if this was the case, the competitor countries' shares in the unadjusted world export total is shown in the last column of Table 4.6, where "competitors" refers to Hong Kong, Israel, Portugal, Spain, Taiwan, and Yugoslavia. These countries' export compositions in the late 1970s were more similar to Korea's than those of other countries. Interestingly, the competitors' market shares rose in 1979 and 1980 at the time of the second oil crisis, indicating that there was no sudden shift in the world demand away from Korea's main export items. This shows that part of the reason why Korea's market share declined at the time of second oil crisis was weakened export competitiveness vis-à-vis that of its competitors, not just the hike in the international petroleum price.

An intriguing question is whether this decline in Korea's market share at the time of second oil crisis had anything to do with the HCI drive. Put differently, the question is: could Korea's market share have been greater, had there been no HCI drive? This question is essentially counterfactual in nature and cannot be given a definite answer. Natural scientists may conduct an experiment with two groups, namely, a treatment group and a control group, which are exactly the same in all respects except for one treatment, and tell the effect of the treatment by observing the difference between the two groups. It is not possible to have such an experiment in economics.

However, in answering the counterfactual question what comes close to the scientist's experiment is possible, if a country can be found that is very similar to Korea in all respects except for its industrial policy. Fortunately, Taiwan fits this requirement reasonably closely. Among countries with a population of greater than 10 million, Taiwan's population density is the second-highest in the world and Korea's the third-highest, while both are poor in natural resources. In the 1970s the two were at a comparable stage in economic development, except that Taiwan started outward-oriented development in the late 1950s, a few years ahead of Korea. Manufactured goods accounted for most of the two economies' exports; in fact, no other country's commodity composition of exports was closer to Korea's than Taiwan's in the 1970s. Culturally, both Korea and Taiwan had a long tradition of Confucianism.

One big difference was industrial policy: Taiwan also had an industrial targeting policy, but it was not anything like Korea's HCI drive. Taiwan's industrial policy was not as discriminatory and targeting was almost meaningless. According to a reliable observer of Taiwanese industrial policy,

> Although many policies were aimed at specific industries at the very beginning, many of them were soon extended to other industries that asked for the same privileges ... Therefore, many industrial policies became so general that the private sector could develop the industries they thought profitable without bothering too much about the industrial targets of the government.[8]

Figure 4.3 shows in percentage terms Korea's and Taiwan's market shares in OECD member countries' total imports of manufactures from the mid-1970s to 1991. There was little difference between the two economies' market shares in the mid-1970s. Thereafter, Korea's share fell behind Taiwan's: it declined from 1.38 percent in 1978 to 1.29 percent in 1979 and 1.16 percent in 1980. It bounced back in the following years but was still smaller than Taiwan's in the early 1990s. In Figure 4.4, the manufactured goods are divided into two groups: the "HC group" and the "light group", the group definitions being the same for Korea and Taiwan.

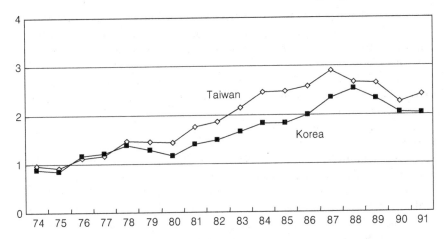

Figure 4.3 Korea's and Taiwan's market share in OECD imports of manufactures, 1974–1991.

Source: Yoo (1997b), Figure 6, p. 22.

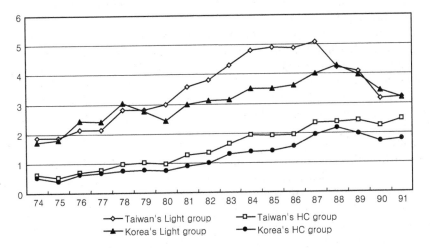

Figure 4.4 Korea's and Taiwan's market share in OECD imports of manufactures, HC group and light group, 1974–1991 (%).

Source: Yoo (1997b), Figure 7, p. 23.

As Figure 4.4 shows, Taiwan's HC group always had a greater market share than Korea's for the period shown in the figure. In contrast, in OECD imports of the light group products, Korea's market share was greater than Taiwan's in 1976, 1977, and 1978 but fell below Taiwan's in the next two years, indicating weakening competitiveness. This decline in export competitiveness of Korea's light group was the reason why Korea's manufactures exports to OECD countries declined in Figure 4.3 and fell behind Taiwan's. Since both countries' exports were mostly destined to OECD member countries in those days and mostly consisted of manufactures, the figure shows the reason why Korea's export performance in the world market deteriorated in the late 1970s and its total exports eventually shrank in 1979.

Does the decline in the light group's export competitiveness have anything to do with the HCI drive? Circumstantial evidence indicates that the answer is "yes". As was discussed in the earlier sections of this chapter, the HCI policy provided the targeted industries with strong policy favors. Since no government can create something out of nothing, the costs of the policy favors had to be borne by someone else in the economy. The directed credits, tax breaks, and trade protection with which the HCI drive provided the HC group meant shrinking credit availability, tax hikes, and higher costs of imported or import-competing inputs for the light group. Thus, the light group's export competitiveness was impaired. This suggests that, had there been no HCI policy, the light group would not have had to bear the costs of the policy favors provided to the HC group, and its competitiveness would not have been impaired. Very likely, Korea's market share in the OECD imports of the light group's manufactured goods in Figure 4.4 would have increased, as Taiwan's did.

In other words, had there been no HCI policy, Korea would not have had to experience the negative growth in exports and investments in the late 1970s and the consequent negative economic growth in 1980. If the HCI drive had continued for a few more years, it could have derailed the economy from its path to a mature, industrialized one. Fortunately, President Park stopped the policy in April 1979. The discontinuation of policy favors to the HC group meant a relief of the burden that the light group was bearing under the HCI drive. Almost immediately, the growth rate of the K/L ratio in the light group bounced back (Table 4.5), and in the following years the exports of the light group regained all of the lost ground of the market share (Figure 4.4).

Nevertheless, the HCI policy is often advocated for the alleged reason that it accomplished what it set out to, that is, the industrial structure in the manufacturing sector shifted away from labor-intensive, simple technology industries to capital-intensive industries with sophisticated technology and, therefore, the benefit was greater than the cost. Indeed, one author asserts that "considering its changing pattern of comparative advantage, Korea had no alternative but to build up HCI" and that "a nation can hardly expect to build a sophisticated industrial structure simply by responding to price signals".[9] Simply put, this amounts to an assertion that, without the HCI policy, the capital-intensive industries of sophisticated production technology could not have developed in Korea. This is an issue of considerable significance, which touches on the question of what lesson to learn regarding the proper role of the government from Korea's development experience. This will be discussed in the second section of the next chapter.

Appendix

Table 4.A1 Effective corporate tax rates (%)

	HCI	Light									
	(1)	(2)	(3)	(4)	(5)	(6)	(7)	(8)	(9)	(10)	(11)
1970	39.2	39.4	38.3	39.9	39.5	41.9	38.8	40.2	41.7	41.6	32.3
1971	34.9	34.7	34.2	33.1	37.3	37.6	33.1	33.7	36.8	38.0	29.2
1972	27.7	29.8	29.5	24.8	28.8	32.7	28.1	28.7	33.5	31.7	24.1
1973	33.5	38.6	33.6	30.8	36.1	38.3	38.0	38.1	40.0	38.9	38.1
1974	29.9	37.7	33.8	33.7	22.3	39.1	35.6	37.5	38.5	37.4	37.8
1975	15.9	52.1	16.9	12.4	18.3	52.8	51.4	52.1	53.0	52.0	51.3
1976	18.0	51.0	19.1	11.9	23.1	52.3	50.4	50.8	51.6	50.8	49.9
1977	17.5	49.5	19.3	11.9	21.3	50.0	48.8	50.0	49.3	50.5	48.6
1978	16.9	48.4	18.2	11.0	21.6	48.9	47.1	48.3	48.6	49.7	47.6
1979	18.3	48.5	21.6	10.6	22.7	49.1	46.8	48.4	49.3	49.3	48.2
1980	18.3	48.8	17.2	15.0	22.8	49.5	48.0	48.7	49.1	48.7	49.0
1981	20.6	51.1	19.5	16.4	26.0	51.3	50.2	52.0	51.4	51.0	50.6
1982	47.1	48.2	47.0	47.5	46.8	48.8	47.2	49.0	48.4	48.1	47.9
1983	40.4	42.2	41.0	40.0	40.3	42.8	41.3	42.9	42.4	42.1	41.9

Source: Kwack (1985), Table 3.5, p. 63.

Notes: The column represents: (1) = a simple average of Columns (3) to (5); (2) = a simple average of Columns (6) to (11); (3) = chemical industries; (4) = primary metal industries; (5) = non-electric and electric machinery industries and transportation equipment industries; (6) = food and beverage industries; (7) = textile, clothing, footwear, and leather industries; (8) = wood product and furniture industries; (9) = pulp and paper, printing, and publishing industries; (10) = non- metal mineral industries; (11) = miscellaneous manufacturing industries.

Table 4.A2 Incremental credit allocation by deposit money banks and the Korea Development Bank (%)

	1973	1974	1975	1976	1977	1978	1979	1980	1981	1982	1983
HC group	35.6	32.2	65.8	60.0	60.7	55.7	58.4	59.8	52.5	68.4	58.3
Light group	64.4	67.8	34.2	40.0	39.3	44.3	41.6	40.2	47.5	31.6	41.7
Sum	100	100	100	100	100	100	100	100	100	100	100

Source: Lee (1991), Table 17.6, p. 446.

Notes

1 This chapter draws upon Yoo (1990, 2012), and Stern, Kim, Perkins, and Yoo (1995), chapter 4.
2 The Office of the Secretary to the President (1976), p. 39. The English translation of the quoted text is the author's.
3 Lee (1991), p. 442.
4 Evaluation Committee of Professors, *Evaluation Report of 5 Year Development Plan*, Seoul: Office of the Prime Minister (various issues).
5 Kwack (1985), pp. 63–65.
6 Kim (1988), pp. 18–25.
7 World Bank (1993), pp. 312–316.
8 Chen (1999), p. 247.
9 Lee (1991), p. 467.

References

Bank of Korea, various years, Economic Statistics Yearbook, Seoul: The Bank of Korea.
Bank of Korea, 1986, Financial System of Our Country, Seoul: The Bank of Korea.
Chen, Pochih, 1999, "The Role of Industrial Policy in Taiwan's Development", in Erik Thorbecke and Henry Y. Wan (eds), *Taiwan's Development Experience: Lessons on Roles of Government and Markets*, Boston, MA: Kluwer.
Economic Planning Board, 1983, Major Statistics of the Korean Economy, Seoul: Economic Planning Board.
Economic Planning Board, 1986, Major Economic Indicators, Seoul: Economic Planning Board.
Evaluation Committee of Professors, 1968–1971, *Evaluation Report of 5 Year Development Plan*, Seoul: Office of the Prime Minister (in Korean).
Kim, Kwang Suk, 1988, *The Economic Impact of Import Liberalization and the Industrial Adjustment Policy*, Seoul: Korea Development Institute (in Korean).
Kwack, Taewon, 1985, *Depreciation and Taxation of Income from Capital*, Seoul: Korea Development Institute (in Korean).
Lee, Suk-Chae, 1991, "The Heavy and Chemical Industries Promotion Plan (1973–79)", in Lee-Jay Cho and Yoon Hyung Kim (eds), *Economic Development in the Republic of Korea: A Policy Perspective* (pp. 431–471), Honolulu, HI: East-West Center.
Ministry of Finance, 1981, Fiscal and Financial Statistics, Seoul: Ministry of Finance.
Office of the Secretary to the President, 1976, *Collection of President Park Chung Hee's Speech*, Vol. 5, Seoul: Daehan Gong-ronsa (in Korean).
Stern, Joseph J., Ji-Hong Kim, Dwight H. Perkins, and Jungho Yoo, 1995, *Industrialization and State: The Korean Heavy and Chemical Industry Drive*, Cambridge, MA: Harvard Institute for International Development.
World Bank, 1993, *The East Asian Miracle*, Washington, DC: The World Bank.
Yoo, Jungho, 1990, "The Industrial Policy of the 1970s and the Evolution of the Manufacturing Sector in Korea", Korea Development Institute Working Paper No. 9017.
Yoo, Jungho, 1997, "The Influence of the World Market Size on the Pace of Industrialization", *KDI Journal of Economic Policy*, Vol. 19, No. 2, pp. 75–157 (in Korean).
Yoo, Jungho, 2012, "The Myth about Korea's Rapid Growth", in Young B. Choi (ed.), *Institutional Economics and National Competitiveness*, London: Routledge.

5   The world market size and the pace of industrialization

5.1 The size of the world market matters

As was discussed in Chapters 2 and 3, Korea's export of manufactured goods began its explosive expansion in 1961, and rapid economic growth and industrialization followed. This and similar experiences in some East Asian countries changed economists' thinking about how international trade affects economic development. The typical pattern of international trade had been that developing countries exported agricultural and/or natural-resource products to and imported manufactured goods from developed countries. Few developing countries had been successful in exporting manufactured goods. Rarely had export expansion been considered a viable industrialization strategy by the economics profession. However, since the export successes of some East Asian countries the opinion of the economics profession underwent a sea change: economists have since then recommended outward-oriented policies for economic development rather than inward-oriented import substitution policies.[1]

There is little doubt that outward-orientation affords a country substantial "gains from trade" that help its economy grow. An interesting question in this regard is whether the size of the world market matters. The theory of international trade often makes the "small country assumption" that the world market is infinitely large. The fact is, the world market has neither been infinitely large nor always of the same size. According to an estimation by Maddison (1995), graphically represented in Figure 5.1, the sum of all countries' exports in 1820, the first year for which the estimate is available, was 7.3 billion in 1990 constant dollars, and it grew to 3,785 billion 1990 constant dollars in 1992, the last year of the estimation, a multiplication of 522 times in 172 years. With such a significant change in the world market size, it would indeed be a big surprise if the gains from trade remained the same regardless of size.

This chapter discusses the relation between the gains from trade and the world market size to see if the rapid pace of Korea's growth and industrialization has something to do with the fact that the world market had grown huge. As mentioned in the previous chapters, it has been the conventional wisdom that "miraculously" rapid growth was achieved because of the Korean government's intervention in the workings of the economy, such as the export promotion

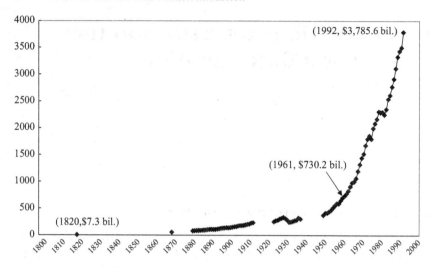

Figure 5.1 Value of world exports, 1820–1992 (billion 1990 dollars).
Source: Yoo (2012), Figure 8.4, p. 163.

policy of the 1960s and the HCI drive of the 1970s. However, as the previous chapters have shown, this view is not supported by the facts and evidence of Korea's growth experience.

5.2 The influence of the size of the world market

In 1961, the year when Korea's rapid export expansion began, Korea's merchandise exports in current dollars were 40.9 million, or 1.8 percent as large compared with the GNP. In that year total world exports were roughly 100 times as large as they had been in 1820.[2] Had the world market in 1961 been of the same size as it was in 1820, Korea's total exports may also have been 1/100-or-so of what they actually were, a tiny fraction of 1 percent compared with GNP. Then, even if Korean exports had increased from the next year as rapidly as they actually did, export could not have been the powerful driving force behind the economy's growth and industrialization it was.[3]

This is not the only way the Korean economy benefitted from the big world market. Productivity gain must also have been considerable. As has long been recognized since the work of Adam Smith (1776), the most important reason for a rise in productivity in an economy is the division of labor, the extent of which depends on the size of the market. This, of course, applies to the international division of labor. For a given export item, a country could export a greater quantity in a large world market than in a small one. Therefore, the bigger the world market, the more of a country's resources will be employed in producing the goods of its comparative advantage, and less in other industries of comparative disadvantage, implying a bigger productivity gain.

Table 5.1 The relative size of the world market to domestic economies

Year	World exports total (million 1990 dollars)	Exports (million 1990 dollars)	Exports/world exports (%)	Exports/ GDP (%)	GDP (million 1990 dollars)
			Korea		
1973	1,797,199	7,894	0.4	24.4	-
			France		
1820	7,255	487	6.7	1.3	38,434
1870	56,247	3,512	6.2	4.9	72,100
			Germany		
1820	7,255	n.a.	n.a.	n.a.	26,349
1870	56,247	6,761	12.0	9.5	71,429
			UK		
1820	7,255	1,125	15.51	3.1	36,232
1870	56,247	12,237	21.76	12.2	100,179

Sources: GDPs for the UK, France, and Germany are from Maddison (2001), Table A1.b. Exports for individual countries are from Maddison (2001), Table F.2. The world export total is from Maddison (1995), Table I.4. The Exports/GDP ratios for Korea are based on values in current-price won.

Notes: Exports refers to merchandise exports, excluding non-factor service exports. n.a. = not available.

How much greater were these "gains from trade" to the Korean economy than to the European economies because of the large size of the world market? It is beyond the scope of this book to estimate the trading countries' gains from trade. However, some statistics are available on the relative size of the world market to national economies. The statistics in Table 5.1, drawn from Maddison (1995, 2001), show the relative size of the world market to the Korean and some European economies. In 1973, when the Korean economy was rapidly growing and industrializing, total world exports were 1,797 billion in 1990 "international" dollars, the currency unit in which the estimates are reported. Korea's merchandise exports in the same year were 7.9 billion in the same currency unit, representing 0.4 percent of total world exports. The exports relative to Korea's GDP in 1973 were 24 percent as large.

In contrast, the world market was much smaller in size relative to European economies. In 1820, when the European economies were in the middle of the First Industrial Revolution, total world exports were 7.3 billion in 1990 international dollars. The UK's exports were 1.1 billion, accounting for as much as 15.5 percent of world exports. However, they were only 3.1 percent as large compared with the UK's GDP. In 1870, roughly a century after the First Industrial Revolution began, the total world exports were 56.2 billion international dollars, and the UK's GDP and exports were 100 billion and 12 billion, respectively. Thus, the UK's exports accounted for 22 percent of the total world exports, but the exports were merely 12 percent as large as the UK's GDP. Similarly, in 1870 France's exports accounted for 6 percent of world exports but were only

5 percent as large as its GDP; in the same year Germany's exports accounted for 12 percent of world exports but were only 9.5 percent as large as its GDP. Thus, during the industrialization process, the relative size of the world market was incomparably bigger to the Korean economy than it was to the UK or other European economies. International trade must have had much greater influence on the growth and industrialization of the Korean economy than it had on the European economies.

This consideration suggests the hypothesis that, for a country engaging in international trade, the bigger the world market, the more rapid the growth of GDP, savings, investments, and capital accumulation. The hypothesis points to the relative size of the world market as one of the main reasons for the "East Asian miracle", by which more than anything else the rapid pace of industrialization is meant. This hypothesis can be put to a statistical test if a measure is available of the length of time that individual countries' industrialization processes took, as estimates of the size of the world market are already available in Maddison (1995).

I put the hypothesis to a simple statistical test by estimating the duration of industrialization in different countries (Yoo, 1997a). The estimation is briefly described here. "Industrialization" is not a well-defined process. In general, it refers to the transformation of a stagnant, agriculture-dominated economy into a dynamic, manufacturing-oriented one, as discussed in Chapter 3. In the process, the importance of the agricultural sector in an economy's output and employ-ment declines and that of the manufacturing sector rises. Hence, it would be commonsensical to estimate the duration of industrialization by referring to the manufacturing sector's share in GNP or employment. However, this was not pos-sible for lack of necessary data—no estimates of the manufacturing or industrial sectors' contribution to GNP exist for the early days of the Industrial Revolution.[4] Nor could the employment share of the manufacturing sector be used for lack of consistent and comparable data across countries and over time. For some coun-tries only statistics on the manufacturing sector were available, while for others only those on the industrial sector were available, which includes electricity, gas, mining, etc. as well as manufacturing.

On the other hand, more consistent statistics were available on the labor force in the agricultural sector, which includes forestry and fisheries as well as agri-culture per se. Because of this availability problem, in estimating the duration of industrialization, the share of the labor force in the agricultural sector was utilized, counting on the regularity with which employment tends to simultan-eously decline in the agricultural sector and increase in the manufacturing sector during the process of industrialization in the experiences of almost all economies. Thus, the "beginning" date of industrialization is defined as the year when the percentage of the labor force in agriculture begins to fall below 50 and the "end" date as the year when it falls below 20. Obviously, the "end" date does not mean that industrialization somehow ended in the year but that the economy may be considered to have become industrialized by then.

Admittedly, this operational definition of the duration of industrialization is arbitrary. For example, by this definition, industrialization in Korea began in 1970 and was accomplished in 1989. Industrialization certainly started earlier in Korea, for the simultaneous fall in the agriculture sector's share in the labor force and the rise in the manufacturing sector's share began in the early 1960s, when the former was greater than 60 percent and the latter less than 10 percent. However, again the operational definition was adhered to because of data availability. If the beginning date of industrialization were to be defined as the year when the share of the labor force in agriculture begins to fall below 60 percent, for example, it would be impossible to pick the beginning date for most European economies; in those years when the earliest statistics are available the share of the labor force in agriculture was already around or below 50 percent in most European countries.

A related difficulty in dating the "beginning" and "end" of industrialization was the paucity of statistics. That the statistics on agriculture's share of the labor force appeared in a certain year did not mean that they became available for every subsequent year. Typically they were available at intervals of ten years or longer. For this reason, to pick the beginning and end dates, linear interpolation or extrapolation was often used. For example, the labor force in the agricultural sector in Belgium was 50.9 percent in 1846 and 46.8 percent in 1856.[5] In this case, it was assumed that the share fell 0.41 percentage points each year during the interval, and the year 1849, when under this assumption the percentage was 50 percent, was picked as the beginning date. For the Netherlands, the share of the labor force in the agricultural sector was already 44.1 percent in 1849 and 37.5 percent in 1859. It was assumed that the share fell by 0.66 percentage points each year during the interval and also in the preceding years. On this ground, the year 1840 was picked as the beginning year of industrialization for the Netherlands.

The beginning and end years thus chosen and the number of years that industrialization took are shown in Columns (A) and (B), respectively, of Table 5.2 for 19 countries. They include all non-socialist countries with a population of more than 10 million that were, by the operational definition, industrialized in the first half of the 1990s. Although the UK, Australia, and New Zealand satisfied this condition, they could not be included in the study because it was not possible to pick the beginning date for these countries, as their labor force in agriculture was already well below 50 percent in the year for which the earliest statistics are available. Also shown in the table for each of the listed countries are total world exports at the beginning year of industrialization in Column (C) and the average annual growth rate of world exports for the duration of industrialization in Column (D).

Using these observations in Table 5.2, I put the hypothesis to a test of ordinary least squares that the bigger the world market, the shorter the duration of industrialization (Yoo, 1997a). Thus, only the industrialized countries were included; the other countries were not. This was to simplify the analysis. The idea behind the statistical test was to see whether the size of the world market quickened the pace of industrialization. In real life there can be many reasons why industrialization begins but may not be completed in a country: civil war, political or social unrest, unfavorable institutions, macroeconomic instabilities, etc. Without independent variables representing most of such conceivable reasons in the regression, if not-yet-industrialized countries were included, the likelihood is practically

Table 5.2 Industrialization experiences

	Beginning and end (A)	Number of years taken (B)	World export total (billion 1990 constant dollars) (C)	Average annual growth rate of world export total (%) (D)
1 Netherlands	1840, 1938	98	139	3.20
2 Denmark	1843, 1957	114	169	3.17
3 Belgium	1849, 1924	75	229	3.26
4 France	1858, 1962	104	311	3.14
5 Ireland	1865, 1979	114	445	3.52
6 USA	1880, 1934	54	792	2.23
7 Germany	1881, 1949	68	815	2.25
8 Canada	1888, 1929	41	1,023	2.93
9 Norway	1891, 1959	68	1,115	2.62
10 Sweden	1906, 1951	45	1,813	1.86
11 Japan	1930, 1969	39	3,120	3.77
12 Italy	1933, 1968	35	2,515	4.56
13 Venezuela	1940, 1972	32	3,151	5.36
14 Spain	1946, 1979	33	3,515	5.87
15 Finland	1946, 1971	25	3,515	6.03
16 Portugal	1952, 1988	36	4,176	5.74
17 Taiwan	1960, 1980	20	7,010	6.10
18 Malaysia	1969, 1995	26	13,233	5.15
19 Korea	1970, 1989	19	14,460	4.48

Sources: The estimates of "World exports total" in (C) are from Maddison (1995). I estimated the beginning and end dates of industrialization in (A) and (B), as explained in the text, on the basis of the estimates of labor force in the agricultural sector, which are from Mitchell (1980, 1983); International Labor Organization, *Yearbook of Labor Statistics*, various issues; and US Bureau of the Census (1973).

zero that the influence of the size of the world market on the pace of industrialization could be estimated with reasonable significance. For this reason, only those countries were included in the test that were, by the operational definition, industrialized in the first half of the 1990s.

The regression result is as follows:

$$lnT = 8.272 - 0.354 lnW - 0.053 RW \ (\bar{R}^2 = 0.87)$$

$$(18.16) \ (7.69) \qquad (1.15)$$

In the equation *ln* stands for natural logarithm, and *T* refers to the number of years that a country's industrialization took (Column (B) of Table 5.2); *W* represents the size of the world market, that is, total world exports at the beginning year of a country's industrialization in Column (C); *RW* represents the average annual growth rate of total world exports in percentage during the period of industrialization in Column (D), a proxy for world economic conditions during the period. As usual, the numbers in the parentheses are the t-value for the coefficient estimated. The estimated coefficients for *lnW* and *RW* both had expected signs,

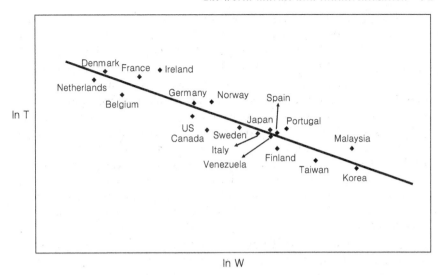

Figure 5.2 World market size and duration of industrialization.
Source: Yoo (1997a), Figure 6, p. 128.

but only the former was estimated with high statistical significance, while the latter was statistically insignificant.

The regression result indicates that indeed the size of the world market had a strong influence on the pace of industrialization. As the size of the world market at the beginning of a country's industrialization increased by 1 percent, the number of years that the country's industrialization took declined by 0.35 percent. Figure 5.2 shows the intercept and the second term of the estimated regression equation, and each country is represented as a point, the coordinates of which are the natural logarithms of W and T, respectively.

The figure plainly shows that the difference in duration of industrialization across countries is mostly explained by the size of the world market. For example, industrialization took the Netherlands and Denmark roughly a century on the one hand and Taiwan and Korea around 20 years on the other. The regression result attributes most of the difference in duration to the difference in W, the size of the world market. Another interesting point readily visible in the figures is that industrialization in such countries as Belgium and Canada took much less time than expected, given the size of the world market, than it did in Taiwan or Korea.

The industrialization experience in some East Asian economies is dubbed a "miracle" primarily because the length of duration was about one-fifth of what it was for the European economies that industrialized earlier. However, this miracle happened not because the industrialization took place in East Asia, but because it began in the second half of the twentieth century, when the size of the world market was more than 100 times bigger than it had been in 1820. In this sense, if it is to be called a miracle, a better expression seems to be the "Twentieth-Century Miracle", rather than the "East Asian Miracle".

Naturally, this raises a question: why did just a handful of developing countries benefit from the big world market in the post-World War II era? A simple and obvious answer is that a country gets gains from trade only if it engages in international trade. The Eastern European countries, which were behind their Western European counterparts in industrialization, did not engage in international trade with the rest of the world for ideological reasons; Latin American countries mostly followed the development strategy of industrialization through import substitution; in Africa few countries seem to have been seriously engaged in international trade—nor were most Asian countries, except for the so-called East Asian Tigers. Singapore and Hong Kong were "entrepot" economies to begin with. Taiwan's development policy had switched from inward-orientation to outward-orientation in the second half of the 1950s.[6] In Korea a major reform of the foreign exchange system in 1961 started the explosive export expansion, as was discussed in Chapter 2. Hence, in the early 1960s the East Asian "Tigers" were practically the only developing economies that were serious about international trade and benefitted from the big world market.

In addition to the big world market, Korea's rapid industrialization was helped by the "unlimited supply of labor", *à la* Lewis (1954). Furthermore, Korea must have benefitted from the fact that the world trading system had become more open and freer in the post-World War II era. In comparison, for the Western European countries, growth of the world market and their domestic economies was going on hand-in-hand, and often military might had to be used to secure markets for a country's exports. For Korea and other newly industrializing countries export success depended more or less only on the competitiveness of their export products in terms of price and quality.

In any case, the main reason for Korea's rapid pace of industrialization and economic growth was the huge size of the world market in the post-World War II era. As shown in Table 5.1 and discussed in the first section of this chapter, the relative size of the world market to the Korean economy was incomparably bigger than it was to the UK's or the economies of other European economies during the First Industrial Revolution. It was for this reason that export was much more powerful a driving force in the transformation of the Korean economy, as was discussed in Chapter 3. The statistical test in this chapter supports this point.

5.3 Upgrading of the industrial structure

The previous section concluded that engaging in international trade in the big world market was the main reason for Korea's rapid industrialization. An integral part of industrialization was a shift in the industrial structure within the manufacturing sector away from labor-intensive, simple technology industries to capital- and technology-intensive industries, which is often referred to as "upgrading". This upgrading is as much an important phenomenon that demands explanation as the rapid pace of industrialization. The widely held view is that the HCI policy of the 1970s upgraded the industrial structure. This view is popular probably because the objective of the policy was upgrading, and this was achieved. The facts about and the reason for the upgrading are discussed in this section.

Table 5.3 shows the gross outputs of the manufacturing sector and of the HC group in 1985 constant prices for those years from 1970 to 2000 for which the Bank of Korea published the input-output (I-O) tables.[7] The gross outputs of an industry in current prices, read off the I-O tables, were converted into constant prices, using the GNP (or GDP) deflators derived in Table 5.A2 in the Appendix to this chapter.[8] As shown in the table, for the 30-year period, the HC group's gross outputs grew at an average rate of 13.4 percent per annum, while the manufacturing sector's gross outputs grew at a rate of 10.1 percent. As a result, the proportion of manufacturing outputs produced by the HC group rose from 26 percent in 1970 to 63 percent in 2000. In other words, in 1970, of the manufacturing sector's gross outputs 74 percent were labor-intensive, simple-technology products; in 2000, of the sector's gross outputs 63 percent were capital-intensive, sophisticated-technology products. Indeed, the industrial structure of the manufacturing sector was upgraded during the 30-year period.

Many observers hold the view that the upgrading was made possible by the HCI policy and that therefore it was worth the cost, as was discussed in Chapter 4. It is also claimed that in general government intervention in the market is necessary for a developing economy to acquire a sophisticated industrial structure, as was noted. Whether or not it was the HCI policy that upgraded the industrial structure is an issue that touches on the role of the government in Korea's development experience. It needs to be examined.

The upgrading of the industrial structure shown in Table 5.3 was, of course, the direct consequence of the HC group's gross outputs having increased more rapidly than the light manufacturing industries' gross outputs. Why did this happen? An industry produces to meet, directly and indirectly, the final demands, of which there are three kinds: consumption, gross fixed capital formation (not counting the inventory change that tends to be small and without a long-term trend), and exports. Table 5.4 shows how much of the HC group's gross outputs are produced in a given year to meet the three components of the final demands. (In estimating Table 5.4, the same procedure was used as that for Table 5.3.) In 1970 the HC group produced 36.0 percent of the gross outputs for consumption, 46.8 percent for fixed capital formation, and 17.2 percent for exports. In 2000, of the HC group's gross outputs 19.7 percent was produced for consumption, 25.6 percent for fixed capital formation, and 54.7 percent for exports. In other words, during the 30-year period from 1970 to 2000, the component of the final demands that increased the HC group's gross outputs most was the export demands. Without exports the HC group's gross outputs in 2000 would have been less than half of what they actually were. That is, the main force behind the upgrading of the industrial structure was the rapid increase in export demands, direct and indirect, for the HC industries' products.

Hence, a critical question regarding the reason for the upgrading is: why did the export demands for the HC industries' products increase as rapidly as shown in Table 5.4? The major policy measures of the HCI drive were "directed credits" with preferential interest rates, tax incentives, and import restrictions, as was discussed in Chapter 4. These policy favors attracted investments to the HC industries and in addition could have lowered their production costs and may have increased the

Table 5.3 Manufacturing gross outputs, 1970–2000 (in billions of 1985 won)

	Manufacturing sector (A)	*HC group (B)*	*Share of HC group (B/A,%)*
1970	16,806.1	4,303.4	25.6
1973	26,840.8	7,522.6	28.0
1975	39,161.0	13,730.3	35.1
1978	55,955.3	20,775.8	37.1
1980	70,775.9	27,746.0	39.2
1983	87,142.9	38,010.1	43.6
1985	95,300.3	41,139.4	43.2
1988	138,400.8	63,046.5	45.6
1990	152,028.8	75,035.4	49.4
1993	176,970.1	96,173.1	54.3
1995	201,225.9	114,816.9	57.1
1998	223,301.2	130,955.9	58.6
2000	297,911.7	188,308.5	63.2
Average annual growth rate (%) (1970–2000)	10.1	13.4	

Table 5.4 Composition of the final demands for the HC group's gross outputs (%)

	Consumption	*Fixed capital formation*	*Exports*
1970	36.0	46.8	17.2
1973	27.9	30.7	41.4
1975	34.7	30.3	35.0
1978	28.6	32.5	38.9
1980	28.1	29.7	42.2
1983	25.9	30.4	43.7
1985	22.6	30.5	47.0
1988	19.9	30.1	50.0
1990	26.2	36.7	37.1
1993	25.3	35.2	39.5
1995	20.3	37.8	41.9
1998	16.5	22.5	61.0
2000	19.7	25.6	54.7

domestic demand for the industries' products for the duration of HCI drive in the 1970s. Were these policy favors also the reason why the HC industries' exports became competitive in the international market and increased rapidly?

Highly relevant to this question is the long-term change in the composition of Korea's exports, shown in Figure 5.3, which is an extension of Figure 2.1 (Chapter 2) to the year 2003. An unmistakable feature in the figure is that the pace of the increase in the export share of SITC 5+7 comprising capital-intensive products of the HC group is very gradual and steady, from under 5 percent in the early 1960s to over 70 percent in the 2000s. Remarkably, the share of the light group (SITC 6+8) in Korea's total exports peaked in 1971 and began to decline

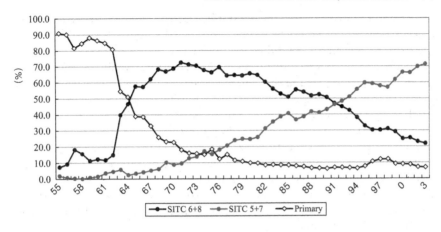

Figure 5.3 Composition of exports, 1955–2003.
Source: Table 5.A3.

after then, while that of the HC group (SITC 5+7) continued to rise. This means that the exports of the HC group were increasing more rapidly than those of the light group after 1971, which, in turn, means that the competitiveness of the HC group in the world market was rising relative to that of the light group even before the HCI drive began.

Why did the exports of the HC group become more competitive? The reason lies in the rapid capital accumulation. As Table 3.6 (Chapter 3) shows, the accumulation of non-residential capital stock per capita in Korea for 13 years from 1966 to 1979 was roughly equivalent to that in the UK for 130 years from 1820 to 1950. The rising capital stock per capita lowered the cost of capital relative to the cost of labor. The consequence was a rapid decline in the production cost of capital-intensive products relative to that of labor-intensive products, a simple Heckscher-Ohlin result in the theory of international trade. This was the main reason why Korea's capital-intensive products became increasingly more competitive in the world market than Korea's labor-intensive products and, in other words, why the share of HC products in Korea's total exports increased from 1971, while that of the light group decreased. Interestingly, in the 1970s when the HCI policy was vigorously pushed, there was no big jump in the HC group's export share in the composition of Korean exports. Moreover, Figure 4.4 (Chapter 4), which compares the market shares of Korea's and Taiwan's HC group in OECD imports of manufactures, shows that the market share of Korea's HC group was always smaller than that of Taiwan's for the duration of the HCI drive and after. The policy favors of the HCI drive apparently had little effect on the competitiveness of the HC group in the world market.

In summary, the immediate reason for the upgrading of Korea's industrial structure was that the HC industries' exports increased much faster than those of the labor-intensive light industries. The HC industries' exports increased faster, because Korea, once a labor-abundant country, was rapidly becoming capital-abundant relative to the rest of the world, thanks to the rapid capital accumulation. Indeed, as was discussed in Chapter 3, the pace of accumulation of non-residential capital stock per capita in Korea during the 1960s, 1970s, and 1980s was incomparably faster than that in the UK or other European countries during the days of their industrialization.[9] This capital accumulation lowered the cost of capital, strengthening the competitiveness of the HC group, while rising wages weakened the competitiveness of the labor-intensive light group.

Why was capital accumulation so rapid in Korea, then? To repeat, the reason was that export was a very powerful driving force behind economic transformation for Korea, thanks to the large size of the world market. As the result, GDP, savings, and investments all grew at a much faster pace in Korea than in the European economies in their days of industrial revolution. It is beyond reasonable doubt that the most important cause of Korea's rapid growth, industrialization, capital accumulation, and upgrading of its industrial structure lay in its trade with the huge world market.

Appendix

Table 5.A1 Concordance between KSIC and I-O industries

Korea Standard Industrial Classification	Input-output table industries					
	1970 I-O (153)	*1975 I-O (164)*	*1980 I-O (162)*	*1985 I-O (161)*	*1990 I-O (163)*	*1995 I-O 2000 I-O (168)*
351 Industrial chemicals	71-75,78	70-79,86	69–72	65–72, exc. 67,68,70	60–68, exc. 63,64,66	60–68, exc. 64,65,66
353 Petroleum refineries	86	91	82–83	79–80	78–79	58–59
371 Iron and steel	95–100	100–104	93–97	90–95	86–92	82–87
372 Non-ferrous metal	101–102	105–106	98–99	96–97	93–94	88–89
381 Fabricated metal products except machinery and equipment	103–105	107–110	100–102	98–100	95–96	90–93
382 Machinery except electrical	106–112	111–116	103–108	101–106	97–101	94–101
383 Electrical and electronic machinery	113–116	117–123	109–115	107–113	102–110	102–110
384 Transport equipment	117–121	124–127	116–120	114–118	114–119	115–121

Table 5.A2 GNP(GDP) deflators, 1970–2000

	GNP (GDP) (in current billion won) (A)	GNP (GDP) (in 1985 constant billion won) (B)	Deflator, 1985 = 1.0 (A/B)
1970	2,735.9	25,608.4	0.1068
1973	5,378.4	33,599.4	0.1601
1975	10,092.2	38,689.8	0.2608
1978	24,225.3	54,599.4	0.4437
1980	372,05.0	55,123.0	0.6749
1983	58,428.4	67,736.0	0.8626
1985	78,088.4	78,088.4	1.0000
1988	126,230.5	111,979.9	1.1273
1990	178,262.1	131,129.6	1.3594
1993	265,517.9	159,009.1	1.6698
1995	348,979.3	180,740.6	1.9922
1998	444,366.5	198,132.4	2.2428
2000	521,959.2	240,208.7	2.1729

Sources: Bank of Korea, *Economic Statistics Yearbook*, various issues.

Note: For those years from 1970 to 1993 estimates of GNP are used. For the later years estimates of GDP are used.

Table 5.A3 Composition of exports, 1955–2003

	Total exports (million dollars)	SITC 6+8 (%)	SITC 5+7 (%)		Total exports (million dollars)	SITC 6+8 (%)	SITC 5+7 (%)
1955	18.0	7.3	1.8	1980	17,504.9	65.6	24.6
1956	24.6	9.2	0.8	1981	21,253.8	64.6	25.8
1957	22.2	18.2	0.3	1982	21,853.4	60.3	31.2
1958	16.5	15.5	0.1	1983	24,445.1	56.0	35.4
1959	19.8	11.2	0.8	1984	29,244.9	52.9	38.7
1960	32.8	12.3	1.5	1985	30,283.1	51.0	40.7
1961	40.9	11.7	3.5	1986	34,714.5	55.5	36.7
1962	54.8	14.8	4.4	1987	47,280.9	54.0	38.5
1963	86.8	39.8	5.7	1988	60,696.4	51.7	41.7
1964	119.1	46.6	2.4	1989	62,377.2	52.4	41.1
1965	175.1	57.6	3.4	1990	65,015.7	50.7	43.2
1966	250.3	57.3	4.1	1991	71,870.1	46.9	46.2
1967	320.2	62.0	5.2	1992	76,631.5	44.9	48.3
1968	455.4	68.2	6.1	1993	82,235.9	42.5	50.9
1969	622.5	66.9	10.1	1994	96,013.2	38.0	55.6
1970	835.2	68.7	8.7	1995	125,058.0	32.7	59.6
1971	1,067.6	72.5	9.6	1996	129,715.1	30.2	59.2
1972	1,624.1	71.2	12.8	1997	136,164.2	30.2	57.9
1973	3,225.0	70.5	13.8	1998	132,313.1	31.0	56.9
1974	4,460.4	67.8	17.1	1999	143,685.5	29.1	61.7
1975	5,081.0	66.3	15.3	2000	172,267.5	24.9	66.2
1976	7,715.3	69.5	18.1	2001	150,439.1	25.3	65.9
1977	10,046.5	64.3	20.6	2002	162,470.5	23.1	69.8
1978	12,710.6	64.6	23.9	2003	193,817.4	21.8	71.2
1979	15,055.5	64.3	24.8				

Source: KOSIS, online service of the National Statistical Office. www.kosis.kr.

Notes

1 See Krueger (1997) for an informative and in-depth discussion of the changes in the opinion of the economics profession.
2 Maddison (1995), Table I.4.
3 This section draws heavily upon Yoo (1997a).
4 Mitchell (1980, 1983) was relied on for statistics on Western European countries.
5 Mitchell (1980).
6 Tsiang (1984).
7 The gross outputs in current prices are converted into constant prices by using the GNP (GDP) deflators calculated in Table 5.A2.
8 The definition of the I-O industries 1, 2, 3, etc. changes over the 30-year period. The concordance between the Korea Standard Industrial Classification (KSIC) in the 1970s and the I-O industries can be found in Table 5.A1.
9 By one estimate, Kwack and Lee (2010), the capital stock for the whole Korean economy multiplied 244 times in real terms from 1960 to 2007, while the number of employees multiplied 3.3 times.

References

Bank of Korea, *Economic Statistics Yearbook*, various issues, Seoul: The Bank of Korea.
Bureau of the Census, US, 1973, *Historical Statistics of the United States, Colonial Times to 1970*, Washington, DC: US Government Printing Office.
International Labor Organization, *Yearbook of Labor Statistics*, various issues.
Krueger, Anne O., 1997, "Trade Policy and Economic Development: How We Learn", *The American Economic Review*, Vol. 87, No. 1, March, pp. 1–22.
Kwack, Sung Yeung and Young Sun Lee, 2010, *Korea's Production Database, 1960–2007*, KIET Occasional Paper No. 79, Seoul.
Lewis, W. Arthur, 1954, "Economic Development with Unlimited Supplies of Labor", *Manchester School*, Vol. 22, No. 2, pp. 139–191.
Maddison, Angus, 1995, *Monitoring the World Economy 1820–1992*, Paris: OECD.
Maddison, Angus, 2001, *The Word Economy: A Millennial Perspective*, Paris: OECD.
Mitchell, Brian R., 1980, *European Historical Statistics, 1750–1975*, London: Macmillan.
Mitchell, Brian R., 1983, *International Historical Statistics: The Americas and Australasia*, London: Macmillan.
Smith, Adam, 1776, *An Inquiry into the Nature and Causes of the Wealth of Nations* (1994 Modern Library Edition), New York: Random House.
Tsiang, Sho-chieh, 1984, "Taiwan's Economic Miracle: Lessons in Economic Development", in Arnold C. Harberger (ed.), *World Economic Growth*, San Francisco, CA: Institute for Contemporary Studies Press.
Yoo, Jungho, 1997a, "The Influence of the World Market Size on the Pace of Industrialization", *KDI Journal of Economic Policy*, Vol. 19, No. 2 (in Korean), pp. 75–157.
Yoo, Jungho, 2012, "The Myth about Korea's Rapid Growth", in Young B. Choi (ed.), *Institutional Economics and National Competitiveness*, London: Routledge.

6 Concluding remarks

How can we explain Korea's rapid growth and industrialization? What was the government's role in the experience? The conventional wisdom characterizes the growth as "government-led".[1] At the macro level the Korean government contributed much to the economy's rapid growth by providing a stable macroeconomic environment, investing in infrastructure and human resources, maintaining an outward orientation in economic policies, and so on. At the industry level, however, the role of the government was not similarly positive. It implemented policies that heavily intervened in the market and altered outcomes. If by "government-led" it is meant that the Korean "miracle" was possible because the government directed economic activities and cajoled the private sector through its interventionist policies, this is misleading.

An outstanding example of interventionist policy was export promotion in the 1960s. According to the conventional wisdom, Korea's rapid export expansion, which was the main driving force behind the economy's rapid growth and industrialization, was possible because of the government's export promotion from the mid-1960s. However, rapid export expansion began in 1961, as Chapter 2 has shown, and the export promotion policy that began in the mid-1960s could not have started it. Rather, the export promotion policy was inspired by the beginning of rapid export expansion. The Korean economy had comparative advantage in labor-intensive manufactures, but its full export potential had not been exploited until 1961 because of the distorted foreign exchange system. The official exchange rate had had significantly overvalued the domestic currency and the structure of the multiple foreign exchange rates was extremely complicated. As soon as this impediment was removed by major reform of the system in 1961, the economy began to realize its export potential. New export items of labor-intensive manufactures appeared and their exports expanded explosively, as was discussed in Chapter 2.

Rapid export expansion continued in the following decades. What was the role of the export promotion policy that began in the mid-1960s? Even after implementation of the export promotion policy the Korean government maintained a protectionist import policy, and it remained so until the early 1980s. Thus, in the 1960s and 1970s the Korean government was simultaneously pursuing an export promotion policy and a protectionist import policy, the consequence being that export promotion offset the export-depressing effects of protectionism, as was discussed in Chapter 2. In other words, export production was carried out in a free trade-like environment. Hence, it is misleading to say that the export promotion policy was the reason for Korea's export success. If there had been no protectionist policy, export promotion may not have been necessary.

Another outstanding example of interventionist policy was the HCI drive of the 1970s, the goal of which was the development of capital-intensive, sophisticated-technology industries. The conventional wisdom holds that the policy was a success, for it achieved its objective of building the heavy and chemical industries that could compete in the world market, although it entailed the cost of resource misallocation, low capacity utilization, shortage of daily necessities, and so on. Often cited as the supporting evidence of this view is the rapid increase in Korea's export of capital-intensive manufactures in the 1980s. The conventional wisdom seems to be based on an implicit assumption that an industry cannot start and grow without government assistance. However, the fact is that an industry starts and grows in a market economy, if it is profitable, with or without government assistance. Moreover, as was discussed in Chapter 4, the HCI policy weakened the competitiveness of Korean exports in the world market and exports shrank in real terms, leading to the negative growth of the economy in 1980. It was fortunate for the Korean economy that the policy was ended by President Park Chung Hee in April, 1979.

The very important reason why the heavy and chemical industries grew and became the major export industries in Korea was rapid capital accumulation. As was discussed in Chapter 3, accumulation of per-capita non-residential capital stock in Korea was incomparably more rapid than in the European countries. This is something not to be overlooked or ignored in accounting for the shift in export composition away from simple labor-intensive products to capital-intensive, sophisticated-technology products. The shift was the expected result of an economy becoming capital-abundant, as this lowers the cost of capital while raising the cost of labor. The very rapid accumulation of capital was the reason why Korea's heavy and chemical industries became increasingly more competitive in the world market than the labor-intensive, light-manufacturing industries.

Why did the conventional wisdom on Korea's experience of rapid growth and industrialization become conventional wisdom? The answer, I believe, is that an external factor that greatly boosted the Korean economy's performance has been overlooked: the huge size of the world market. As was discussed in Chapter 5, the world export total was more than 100 times bigger in the early 1960s, when the Korean economy was beginning to industrialize, than when the European economies were in the middle of the First Industrial Revolution. Therefore, during the process of industrialization, the relative size of the world market to the Korean economy was incomparably bigger than it had been to the European economies. For example, in 1973 Korea's total exports were roughly 0.4 percent of total world exports and were 24 percent as large as Korea's GDP. In comparison, UK exports in 1870 accounted for as much as 22 percent of total world exports but were only 12 percent as large as the UK's GDP.

Therefore, to the Korean economy the gains from trade were incomparably greater, and export was incomparably more powerful a driving force of economic transformation than it had been to the UK or other European economies. The consequence was incomparably more rapid economic growth and capital accumulation. This is the secret behind the Korean "miracle"; it was thanks to the huge world market, not to interventionist government policies. The reason why the growth experiences of Korea and other East Asian economies are known as the "East Asian Miracle" is not that the quality of their growth and industrialization was miraculously superior in some sense compared to the European countries' experiences, but that the pace of growth and industrialization was very, very rapid. This rapid pace is mostly explained by the size of the world market, as was discussed in Chapter 5.

In the Korean context, there seems to be another reason why the conventional wisdom tends to attribute the country's rapid growth and industrialization to interventionist policies such as export promotion or the HCI drive. The transformation of Korea from one of the poorest countries in the world into a dynamic, newly industrializing economy took place in the 1960s and 1970s. This period exactly coincides with the period during which President Park Chung Hee was in power, whose strong government implemented highly interventionist policies. Apparently, many observers are persuaded that whatever policies the government implemented under President Park transformed the economy, which is logically a proof of causality by association. For this reason, the phrase "development dictatorship", suggesting that dictatorship was somehow helpful for rapid growth, was once widely used in discussing Korea's experience. To see how misleading the thought is, one need only recognize that there are many countries in the world ruled by dictators whose economies are going nowhere.

In short, in the Korean experience of rapid growth and industrialization one can find no evidence that supports the view that the government's interventionist policies made the "miracle" happen. Rather, the Korean economy's rapid growth and industrialization may better be understood as a process whereby the economy realized its huge potential. This potential, untapped until the early 1960s, was so large because of the abundance of a relatively well-educated labor force on the one hand and a huge world market on the other. As soon as the impediments to international trade were removed in the early 1960s, explosive export expansion immediately followed, capital accumulation ensued, and the economy began to fulfill its potential.

The important lesson from Korea's development experience is that a market economy realizes its potential on its own, given an institutional and policy environment that presents no impediments to the workings of the market forces. The policy priority for a developing country aspiring to develop a mature and industrialized economy should be the identification and removal of impediments, of which there can be many, different to different countries. In addition, it cannot be emphasized too strongly that outward orientation needs to be maintained in institutions and policies. Today's world market is simply too huge to ignore, and any country that does not take international trade seriously is bound to fall behind others.

Note

1 For example, Kim and Leipziger (1993) titled their work "Korea: A Case of Government-Led Development".

Reference

Kim, Kihwan and Danny M. Leipziger, 1993, *Korea: A Case of Government-Led Development*, Washington, DC: World Bank.

Bibliography

Amsden, Alice H., 1989, *Asia's Next Giant: South Korea and Late Industrialization*, New York: Oxford University Press.

Bank of Korea, various issues, *Economic Statistics Yearbook*, Seoul: The Bank of Korea.

Bank of Korea, Research Department, 1960, "Changes in Official Exchange Rate", *Bank of Korea Research Monthly*, December, Vol. 14, pp. 12–24 (in Korean).

Bureau of the Census, US, 1973, *Historical Statistics of the United States, Colonial Times to 1970*, Washington, DC: US Government Printing Office.

Chen, Pochih, 1999, "The Role of Industrial Policy in Taiwan's Development", in Erick Thorbecke and Henry Wan (eds), *Taiwan's Development Experience: Lessons on Roles of Government and Markets* (pp. 231–248), Boston, MA: Kluwer.

Cho, Lee-Jay and Yoon Hyung Kim (eds), 1991, *Economic Development in the Republic of Korea: A Policy Perspective*, Honolulu, HI: East-West Center.

Cole, David C. and Princeton N. Lyman, 1971, *Korean Development: The Interplay of Politics and Economics*, Cambridge, MA: Harvard University Press.

Cole, David C. and Yung Chul Park, 1983, Financial Development in Korea, 1945–1978, Cambridge, MA: Council on East Asian Studies, Harvard University.

Economic Planning Board, 1961, *The First 5-Year Economic Development Plan 1962–1966*, Seoul: Economic Planning Board (in Korean).

Economic Planning Board, 1964, *The First 5-Year Economic Development Plan, Revised*, Seoul: Economic Planning Board (in Korean).

Evaluation Committee of Professors, 1968–1971 *Evaluation Report of 5 Year Development Plan*, Seoul: Office of the Prime Minister (in Korean).

Frank, Charles R., Jr., Kwang Suk Kim, and Larry E. Westphal, 1975, *Foreign Trade Regimes and Economic Development: South Korea*, New York: National Bureau of Economic Research.

Hong, Wontack, 1979, *Trade, Distortions and Employment Growth in Korea*, Seoul: Korea Development Institute.

Hong, Wontack, and Anne O. Krueger (eds), 1975, *Trade and Development in Korea*, Seoul: KDI.

Joh, Sung Wook, 1999, "Profitability of Korean Firms before the 1997 Economic Crisis", *KDI Journal of Economic Policy*, December, Vol. 21, No. 2, pp. 3–54.

Kang, Gwang-ha, Younghoon Rhee and Sang-oh Choi, 2008, *Policy Decision Making System in the Rapid Growth Period*, Seoul: Korea Development Institute (in Korean).

Kim, Chung-yum, 2011, *From Hope to Despair: Economic Policymaking in Korea 1945–1979* (pp. 19–45), Seoul: Korea Development Institute.

Kim, Kihwan and Danny M. Leipziger, 1993, *Korea: A Case of Government-Led Development*, Washington, DC: World Bank.

Kim, Kwang Suk, 1975, "Outward-Looking Industrialization Strategy: The Case of Korea", in Hong Wontack, and Anne O. Krueger (eds), *Trade and Development in Korea* (pp. 19–45), Seoul: Korea Development Institute.

Kim, Kwang Suk, 1988, *The Economic Impact of Import Liberalization and the Industrial Adjustment Policy*, Seoul: Korea Development Institute (in Korean).

Kim, Kwang Suk, 1991, "Part I: Korea", in D. Papageorgiou, M. Michaely, and A. M. Choksi (eds), *Liberalizing Foreign Trade* (pp. 1–132), Cambridge, MA: Basil Blackwell.

Kim, Kwang Suk and Michael Roemer, 1979, *Growth and Structural Transformation*, Cambridge, MA: Council on East Asian Studies, Harvard University.

Kim, Kwang Suk and Larry E. Westphal, 1976, *Korea's Foreign Exchange and Trade Regimes*, Seoul: Korea Development Institute (in Korean).

Krueger, Anne O., 1979, *The Developmental Role of the Foreign Sector and Aid*, Cambridge, MA: Council on East Asian Studies, Harvard University.

Krueger, Anne O., 1997, "Trade Policy and Economic Development: How We Learn", *American Economic Review*, Vol. 87, No. 1, pp. 1–22.

Krueger, Anne O., 2010, "What Accounts for the Korean Economic Miracle?", paper read at the conference "The Korean Economy: Six Decades of Growth and Development", Seoul, August 30.

Krueger, Anne O. and Jungho Yoo, 2002, "Falling Profitability, Higher Borrowing Costs, and Chaebol Finances during the Korean Crisis", in David T. Coe and Se-Jik Kim (eds), *Korean Crisis and Recovery*, Washignton, DC: IMF.

Kuznets, Simon, 1966, *Modern Economic Growth: Rates, Structure, and Spread*, New Haven, CT: Yale University Press.

Kuznets, Simon, 1973, "Modern Economic Growth: Findings and Reflections", *American Economic Review*, Vol. 63, No. 3, pp. 247–258.

Kwack, Taewon, 1985, *Depreciation and Taxation of Income from Capital*, Seoul: Korea Development Institute (in Korean).

Lee, Suk-Chae, 1991, "The Heavy and Chemical Industries Promotion Plan (1973–79)", in Cho, Lee-Jay and Yoon Hyung Kim (eds), *Economic Development in the Republic of Korea: A Policy Perspective* (431–472), Honolulu, HI: East-West Center.

Lewis, W. Arthur, 1954, "Economic Development with Unlimited Supplies of Labor", *Manchester School*, Vol. 72, No. 6, pp. 712–723.

Maddison, Angus, 1995a, *Explaining the Economic Performance of Nations: Essays in Time and Space*, Aldershot: Edward Elgar.

Maddison, Angus, 1995b, *Monitoring the World Economy 1820–1992*, Paris: OECD.

Maddison, Angus, 2001, *The Word Economy: A Millennial Perspective*, Paris: OECD.

Ministry of Commerce and Industry, 1988, *40 Years of Export Promotion*, Seoul: Ministry of Commerce and Industry.

Mitchell, Brian R., 1980, *European Historical Statistics, 1750–1975*, New York: Facts on File.

Mitchell, Brian R., 1983, *International Historical Statistics: The Americas and Australasia*, London: Macmillan.

Office of the Sectary to the President, 1976, *Collection of President Park Chung-Hee's Speeches*, Vol. 5, Seoul: Daehan Gongron-sa (in Korean).

Olson, Mancur, 1996, "Big Bills Are Left on the Sidewalk: Why Some Nations Are Rich, and Others Poor", *Journal of Economic Perspectives*, Vol. 10, No. 2, pp. 3–24.

Park, Pil Soo, 1983, "The Incentive Schemes for Export Promotion", presented at the International Forum on Trade Promotion and Industrial Adjustment, Seoul, September 6–15.

Pyo, Hak K., 1998, *Estimates of Fixed Reproducible Tangible Assets in the Republic of Korea, 1954–1996*, Seoul: Korea Institute of Public Finance.

Rodrik, Dani, 1995, "Getting Interventions Right: How South Korea and Taiwan Grew Rich", *Economic Policy*, Vol. 20, pp. 55–107.

Smith, Adam, 1776, *An Inquiry into the Nature and Causes of the Wealth of Nations*. 1994 Modern Library Edition, New York: Random House.

Stern, Kim and Yoo Perkins, 1995, *Industrialization and State: The Korean Heavy and Chemical Industry Drive*, Cambridge, MA: Harvard Institute for International Development.

Westphal, Larry E. and Kwang Suk Kim, 1982, "Korea", in Bela Balassa and Associates (eds), *Development Strategies in Semi-industrial Economies* (pp. 212–279), Baltimore, MD: Johns Hopkins University Press.

World Bank, 1993, *The East Asian Miracle*, Washington, DC: The World Bank.

Yoo, Jungho, 1990, "The Industrial Policy of the 1970s and the Evolution of the Manufacturing Sector in Korea", KDI Working Paper No. 9017, Seoul, Korea Development Institute.

Yoo, Jungho, 1997a, "The Influence of the World Market Size on the Pace of Industrialization", *KDI Journal of Economic Policy*, Vol. 19, No. 2, pp. 73–157 (in Korean).

Yoo, Jungho, 1997b, "Neoclassical versus Revisionist View of Korean Economic Growth", Development Discussion Paper No. 588, Harvard Institute for International Development, Harvard University.

Yoo, Jungho, 2012, "The Myth about Korea's Rapid Growth", in Young B. Choi (ed.), *Institutional Economics and National Competitiveness* (pp. 154–166), London: Routledge.

Yoo, Jungho, 2017, "Korea's Rapid Export Expansion in the 1960s: How It Began", *KDI Journal of Economic Policy*, Vol. 39, No. 2, pp. 1–23.

Yoo, Yoon-Ha, 2008, "The East Asian Miracle: Is It Export-led or Investment-led?", Working Paper 08-07, Seoul, KDI School of Public Policy and Management.

Index

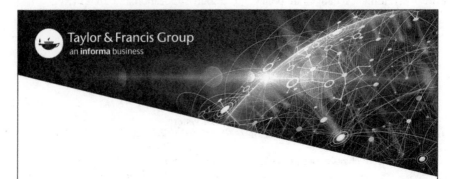